# SERVING PRESIDENTS AND ROYALS:
## A MEMOIR OF AN AFRICAN CHEF

By Yaa Asabea Owusu and Francis Kodjo Andoh-Otoo

Copyright © 2022 Penman Publishing Limited

All rights reserved. No parts of this publication may be reproduced, distributed, or transmitted in any form or by any means, including photocopying, recording, or other electronic or mechanical methods, without the prior written permission of the publisher or Author, Francis Kodjo Andoh-Otoo or the publishers, Penman Publishing ltd, except for the use of brief quotations in a book review.

**ISBN: 978 – 9988 – 3 – 4519 – 8**

**Written by:** Yaa Asabea Owusu
**Narrated by:** Francis Kodjo Andoh-Otoo
**Published by** Penman Publishing Limited
Penman.info@gmail.com
+233242487703 / +233244772813
Penmanonline.com with Fransarcatering.com

**Edited** : Amy Yeboah Quarkume, PhD. Associate professor at Howard University and Gabriel Myers Hansen

**Cover Design**: Reins Films
**Illustrated**: Ebenezer Adu Larbi

# DEDICATION

To my late brother, Benjamin Kwesi Andoh-Otoo, who suffered in silence while I strenuously pursued success. My Mother, Rtd. Lt Col Victoria Larko Abadji, who bent over backwards to cater for her children.

My Feisty loyal and dedicated wife, who stood by me through the wildest storm to support my ideas disregarding the absurdity.

To The Apostle General, Reverend Sam Korankye Ankrah and Reverend Mrs. Rita Korankye Ankrah — the vessels of God under whose guidance I navigated the course of life and my career.

To Apostle Emmanuel Agormerda, for shepherding and sustaining my faith and relationship with God over the past decade in the United States of America.

To my three children; Cecelia, Gilbert and Francis Otoo Jnr, Who suffered varying levels of abandonment whilst I focused entirely on working hard to keep poverty at bay.

To all Millennial Chefs who are interested in varieties of Cuisines, through the narration of stories from my childhood, my rise to relevance in the global cuisine community and how cooking established the centre of my Family's dynamic, It is my prayer that you fetch from the well of my story for refreshment as you pursue your own unique journey to success

# ACKNOWLEDGMENTS

*This is the Lord's doing and it is marvelous in our eyes.*
*Psalm 118:23*

Everything I had hoped to be, with all that I have become; I owe it to the Lord God Almighty, The master of all principality and power, in whom I have been able to make it this far. With glory, He has crowned every effort I had put into this half century of my life and has filled it with gladness. This memoir would not have been possible without the constant show of support from the people I have been surrounded by. Without the prayers of my mother, Mama Victoria Abadji, I would not have grown to become the Chef I am. Her unconditional love for my family goes to depict pride and confidence in me. Whenever I had felt inadequate, she was swift to revive me with reminders from the scriptures — about how I am capable of doing all things with the strength of God.

My wife, my partner, my best friend and confidante, with whom I have shared the adventures of life; The young Miss Sarah Vroom of Golden Tulip, who somehow, coerced me into becoming a better man deserving of her heart. The Now Mrs. Sarah Otoo, who had said yes to a boy with an empty pocket and agreeing to embark on this thing called life with that same boy who was still finding himself. I appreciate you for standing by me all these years, though you had every reason to bolt, given our dire financial situation in the beginning. Two decades gone, baby,
we have forever more to go.

To my late older brother, my shield from since I could recite the alphabets. The best brother a boy could ever ask for. I give you your flowers today for a every smile you put on my face, for every time you were at my defense. Joining forces with me to beat the scorn and bully in our own little world will forever hold a special place in my heart. To say I miss you is an understatement. It kills me knowing that you died without having and raising a family of your own. A place where you would have probably found the peace and community, you had craved all your life. Keep resting brother…in the perfect peace and calm you had wanted.

I feel so blessed and highly favored to have been placed under the covering of the Apostle General and founder of the Royal House chapel, Ahenfie, Reverend Sam Korankye Ankrah and his wife, Mama Rita Korankye Ankrah for their prayers — constant prayers and counsel which has and continues to make me a light unto others. Papa, Mama, God bless you for opening your arms and the doors of your home to me and my family, and for calling us yours as well. Like a son tells a father; I hope I continue to make you proud.

Then there is Ambassador Martha Pobee, the woman who implanted in me, the true art diplomacy. The woman who tirelessly fought till I found my permanent space at the embassy of Ghana, I would not be able to function fully as an International Executive chef and a business owner if it wasn't for your unwavering faith in my person and abilities. Your energy, passion and enthusiasm for work and the things of God challenges me to be and do better every single day. You have taught me that family is not as they say — a group of people related by blood but rather, one related and connected by soul. Thank you for placing me on a platform upon which my gifts continues to flow freely.

To Miss Laine and all members of the catering department of Accra Polytechnic, whom I have neither seen nor heard from in years, your all inclusive catering gigs brought me steps closer to realizing what it was like to run a full time business. Your keenness on punctuality and self grooming had unknowingly set the fount for what would become a life transforming career.

Maplewood Park Place, how do I forget the establishment which continues to hold me down away from Fransar and the Embassy of Ghana? To the management for allowing me the freedom to incorporate my ideas into meeting and knitting the nutritional needs of our clients into our daily menu.

To the military families at 37 military barracks, the single mothers struggling to raise opinionated boys and girls with wild dreams, please, keep giving them reasons to be hopeful, continue fueling their dreams with your support, no matter how small. The future of the world as we see it, is dependent on how these young ones emerge from those uncertain seasons. Also to the ever growing consumers and clients of Fransar Catering Services, in all of North America, to say we appreciate you is an understatement. I, personally, cherish you for constantly entrusting your welfare into our care. With every food pack, with every event you put us on, we cannot unhear the reiterations of your confidence and value for our services. Special thanks to everyone who contributed to making this memoir a success. To Miss Asabea Owusu and her publishing team at Penman Publishing for collaborating on making the birth of this book a success.

# CONTENT

Foreword by Reverend Sam Korankye Ankrah

Part 1   The Beginning
Part 2   Against all Odds
Part 3   New beginnings
Part 4   The Journey continues

**Part 1:**
Chapter 1 ........................................................................ 2
Chapter 2 ....................................................................... 14
Chapter 3 ....................................................................... 26
Chapter 4 ....................................................................... 38
Chapter 5 ....................................................................... 53

**Part 2:**
Chapter 6 ....................................................................... 77
Chapter 7 ....................................................................... 86
Chapter 8 ....................................................................... 94
Chapter 9 ..................................................................... 103
Chapter 10 ................................................................... 114

**Part 3:**
Chapter 11 ................................................................... 132
Chapter 12 ................................................................... 142
Chapter 13 ................................................................... 155
Chapter 14 ................................................................... 173
Chapter 15 ................................................................... 183

Part 4:
Chapter 16 ............................................................. 212
Chapter 17 ............................................................. 224
Chapter 18 ............................................................. 234
Chapter 19 ............................................................. 241
Chapter 20 ............................................................. 252
Chapter 21 ............................................................. 260

# FOREWORD

There's something to be said about Chef Francis' humility, passion and fear of God. These attributes, rare and noble, and which I observed about him upon our first meeting in 2002, have remained with me ever since, strengthening our bond as father and son.

For anyone even slightly familiar with his craft and ethic, Francis' work is not just a meal for the stomach, but also, food for the soul. A singular dedication honed over decades ensures this. It is no wonder, then, that he stands distinguished among his contemporaries.

Proverbs 18: 16 talks about how far a man's gift can take him. Francis's gift has secured him audience before some of the most notable names of these times, including multiple Ghanaian heads of state, former US president Bill Clinton, and the revered South African priest and activist Desmond Tutu.

Watching Francis's path fills me with extreme joy and pride. As a father, I am honored to be a part of his journey and, together with my wife, be positioned by God to offer spiritual guidance and support.

He has been selfless enough to give us a glimpse of what it took for him to sail through the storms he faced in his career and family to arrive at his purposed destination. He's had the desire for years to share the story of how a low-born from Accra could beat the raging odds life flung at him to embrace God's favor and continually accomplish great heights.

The desire to share his story remained a dream until seven years ago, he felt strongly that it was imperative for everyone, especially in a generation plagued by an undying obsession for shortcuts to success. This book, I believe, will give them a new orientation, re-aligning them to make the best of their lives.

You will notice, as you flip through the enthralling pages of this book, that Francis has been persistent in his pursuit of success. As a patient and relentless tastemaker, Francis has, through a life of diligent service, established himself as a beacon of hope, a pathfinder and a testament to what it means for men to see one's good works, and glorify his Father in heaven, as Mathew 5: 16 highlights.

His passion on the job has afforded the kind of success the Bible highlights in Proverbs 22:29: *"Seest thou a man diligent in his business? He shall stand before kings; He shall not stand before mean men. He will not fail."*

Chef Francis Otoo has stood tall in his field of practice with professionalism and an amazing attitude. His single mindedness and confidence in trying new things are worth emulating.

Thus, it is my deep conviction that this memoir will not only challenge other stakeholders in the culinary fraternity but spark positive disruptions in various other fields. Whatever calling you find yourself in as a pastor, politician or entrepreneur.

I implore readers to learn from Francis' unbroken zeal, belief and professionalism, as these are proven tenets to obtaining the successful results we seek in our various fields.

*- By the Apostle General,*
*Reverend Sam Korankye Ankrah,*
*Royal House Chapel International.*

# Part 1

# The Beginning

# Chapter 1

# Chapter 1

I spent most of my childhood with my grandmother, the dark, brown-eyed Mrs Janet Maku Abadji at South Labadi Estates. She was a disciplinarian who did everything in her capacity to raise my older brother Benjamin Kwesi Andoh and me in the ways of the Lord while equipping us with African culinary skills. She would often say, "With these skills, when you get married one day and your wives are being bluffs, you will never go hungry." Grandma Maku used to bake for some people in the neighbourhood. All of her children, except my mother, who was mostly out of town on military assignments, took a keen interest in the craft because of her. She was the real definition of an African woman. A Jill of all trades who, peddled foodstuffs including gari (cassava flakes), charcoal and plantain, among others. If an item was in demand, she quickly made a trade switch to make it available to her customers. My brother and I were not spared from her business expeditions. We hawked anything she brought home on the streets. If you desired a restful sleep in Grandma Maku's house, you had to pay heed to every instruction she gave regarding her dear commodities. Play on the contrary and you would be served a cold bowl of scolding or a good old Ghanaian spanking mixed with your own tears.

One Saturday, as was the ritual, she sent me to hawk a tray of gari. As I strolled on the road overlooking the beach, I spotted a group of my peers playing soccer and thought it would be a great time to display my skills. Ah, the beach, where local fishermen paraded their canoes as if it were a pageant, the women with their *apanpan* well-balanced on their laps to display fresh catches purchased from the fishermen. The white sand that guarded the lush blue ocean, together with the streaks of the orange sun had conspired to create the perfect backdrop for the game.

I made my way down the shore, handing over my tray to some friends among the spectators–careless pre-teens who ended up soiling the product with sand. As I made my way back home, I was troubled, painfully aware of what awaited me at home. The only way to get away with it was to first preen my clothes and get rid of all evidence that I had gone to the beach. Secondly, I had to ensure that I accounted correctly for all items sold. Finally, I was going to stay quiet about everything that occurred. Initially, my plan seemed to have worked. At dinner time, I was well fed with Grandma Maku's signature palm nut soup, laced with mushrooms and tuna, locally referred to as *'poku'*. I took a cold bath soon after and jumped straight into bed, even without saying a prayer. As I embraced the chills of the dawn breeze on the small mattress I shared with my brother, I felt a sharp flash of pain on my buttocks. I was jerked awaked. There stood Grandma, towering over me, whip in hand. While I slept, Grandma somehow discovered the result of my escapades. She gave me a good lashing, before making her way to the bathroom to prepare for her journey to *Makola* (a central market square in Accra). To this day, I can't fathom how she found out about the incident. Those moments with Grandma's punishment were terrifying. Weirdly, it strengthened our bond.

My grandfather, Gilbert Baah Abadji believed in counselling as a form of discipline. This sent him to my rescue whenever Grandma cracked her dawn whip on our little behinds to save us some pain.

Aunty Ruby Abadji, the seventh and last of my mother's siblings, also lived in South Labadi Estates with us. She assumed the role of a mother with ease whenever she attended to the needs of Ben and me in the smallest ways she could. When I was born, she volunteered to care for me. With my body strapped tightly on her back with a cloth, she would get down to assist my mum with household chores and to cater for us. Aunty Ruby was a great cook like her mother, my grandmother. In the kitchen, she would whip up authentic Ghanaian delicacies for the household with me as her assistant. As one of the first few people to discover my passion for cooking, Aunt Ruby would pull out a wooden stool next to hers for me, patiently taking me through the rudiments of preparing meals. 'Joojo, fetch me the pepper in the fridge, she would say in such moments. 'Joojo, slice the onions this way" demonstrating with expert hands. My culinary skills were at her mercy as she polished them carefully and with love. Ben did not have such a relationship with her — the expressive boy who never hesitated to air his opinions — revealed an unusual soft-spoken nature in her presence. Despite this, she was revered by him. The sound of Grandma's whips were whistles in comparison to the roaring voice Aunty Ruby would make in an attempt to discourage her from deepening our misery. Each whip was a twist in her womb.

"Maa, do you want to kill somebody's children?" she'd cry. "Allow me to discipline them."

"No no no, you've already done enough," she would respond, pulling us away.

We were privileged to have been surrounded by other members of our extended family in my grandparents' house, including cousins from well-to-do homes who could afford the luxury of shuffling between Ghana and the UK. Whenever they came back home, it felt like Santa Claus had come to town. They would come bearing gifts of all kinds, including a variety of cookies and candies for all the kids in the family. Grandma always found a way to conceal them but Ben and I, blessed with the skills of police inspectors, would always rescue those cookies and candies from the deepest place in Grandma's bag or wherever she hid them. To a modern-day child, cookies and candies are not so much of a big deal, probably the least of items they'd die for. Unlike in my day, when they were rarely seen until there was some sort of festive occasion. Sometimes it would come down to stealing these items prior to them being shared among the kids just to have more to myself. I shared a strong bond with Benjamin. We had the kind of healthy sibling relationship where we would often cover up for each other's faults. Due to his dwarfism, my grandparents would naturally shift all his mischief on me and topped it off with a punishment for two whenever we both got into or created any form of trouble. "We are equals," I would mutter under my breath whenever he was given one of those special treatments. His diminutive stature did not make him a weakling to me. Ben and I shared in each other's aspirations. We were free to dream. He aspired to be an engineer while I, on the other hand, hoped to be a doctor. We got ourselves some toys aligning with our dreams and acted out our roles during after-school playtime. Ben had it coming whenever he would touch my hospital toys. it was almost like a ritual to start a fight. "What has an engineer got to do in a doctor's field?" I'd ask, shoving him to the side. He would then grab me by the legs, throw me to the floor and land several blows on my face. His stature was misleading. Ben was quite heavy and strong. Still, I'd turn over with all my might to administer a taste of his medicine to him. We would crown our quarrels with a territorial demarcation of either the bed we shared or the area we kept our clothes. And we dared not to cross those boundaries till our arguments died with the night. Though mostly agitating, those sparks added to the essence of my childhood. *Ah!* I recall the 1998 Trade Fair Exhibition held at La in Ghana. At the time, My Brother and I had gone back to live with our mum at 37 Military housing. Sensing our innermost desire, my mother sounded a strong warning to deter us from attending the highly publicised trade exhibition, yet, the operation 'Go to the Trade Fair Centre' was still on our little minds. The road was clear. With no money in our possession, we sneaked out of the house to the venue for an adventure. It was the first of its kind in our day and certainly not to be missed. In addition, we could not afford to look stupid among our friends at school the next day when memories of the event were being relived.

If you've never been to a trade fair in Ghana, let me fill you in. It typically comprised hundreds of vendors neatly lined up in the many pavilions showcasing goods ranging from food to clothing, horticultural accessories etc. The sound of good music blended with the loud voices of curious window shoppers like me who looked on eagerly as they moved from one vendor to the other to sample products on display. We were simply high off the satisfaction of being surrounded by people from all walks of life and race. For two broke boys, we did have a lot of fun wandering about. Looking back, I believe we were just little boys capitalising on what felt like a rare opportunity to be around a tiny percentile of the affluent in Ghana. We checked the time and it was 4 am. We had overindulged. Though we were exhausted to walk all the way home, it was the sole option on the table — our feet were worn out from all the gallivanting we had done. Ben led the way with me in tow, with our backs hunched and our eyes rolling from side to side like thieves in the night, we made our way to the living room as quickly and quietly as we could. Lo and behold! There was our mother, seated on the double cushion sofa in our living room with her arms folded. *Bueii* We had brought this upon ourselves. As for what happened next, I'll leave that to your imagination.

At South Labadi, our neighbours were like family. I fondly recall playing with kids of the Nkansahs who lived next door, and the Torgbor family, who lived across the street. We co-existed in so much love, respect and harmony that, all neighbours were at liberty to discipline naughty kids from other homes who misbehaved at play time in their residence. In my case, it was often topped up with some extra whipping from Grandma. When it rained heavily, the boys in the neighbourhood would craft tiny boats out of paper to set sail in the choked clear water gutters. The fastest sailor was adjudged the winner on the day. On some days, we would all sneak out to the beach for a swim without notifying our families. It was always a thrill till we were caught by loud-mouthed neighbours who sounded the alarm to summon our respective families with hopes of seeing us beaten for their viewing pleasure. We did almost everything together with the neighbourhood kids, except eat at their homes. My grandparents were firm to counsel us against eating from other people's homes. They preached a gospel we grew to abide by. They'd say: *"This world is unpredictable. You never know who might be up against you so, you're better off eating from your own home. Some people find it harder to make ends meet, the little sustenance they'd put on their table should not be your target meal for the day. Please, you boys should stay content and manage with every provision made for you."*
We would listen placidly and respond in unison, *"Yooo!"*
Of course, we were kids, we slacked on some days. On days when the neighbours would prepare spicy *nane* (pig feet), I would provoke the wrath of my grandmother. *Nane* was

forbidden in our home due to religious beliefs. Whenever its aroma wafted about in the atmosphere, my little nose would twitch in its direction till I sat at the table of whoever served it. Our little street at South Labadi was one of togetherness, which also offered a sense of identity and belonging. It was home.

As a barracks boy born in the Eastern Region of Ghana, in 1973 to Rtd. Lt Col Victoria Larko Abadji and Rtd. Lt Col Nicholas Otoo, I thought that life would be smooth-sailing, but the contrary happened. My mother, a single parent, did not depend on her husband for financial support. She was left with the burden of catering for our needs and hers. She singlehandedly trained us to undertake household chores and keep a home spotless. So we were halfway through our home training before relocating to South Labadi to live with our Grandparents. As part of her duties to the Ghana Armed Forces, my mother was mostly on assignments which required a lot of travelling, depriving her of ample time to raise her boys.

Before moving to South Labadi, I had my nursery education at Burma Camp Kindergarten and got enrolled at Burma Camp Complex schools where I spent four of my six years of primary education before transferring to Osu Home School for my common entrance exams and the final two years of elementary school. At school, learning came natural to me, and my performance and conduct were exemplary. I was appointed as class prefect and assistant school prefect simultaneously. At the end of every academic year, the administration organised a speech and prize-giving day ceremony to reward deserving students who performed with excellence. As part of the formalities, all parents of nominated students were invited to the school to sign documents to allow the conferment of honours on their wards. Unfortunately, my mother was on a mission in

Liberia at the time, and hence could not be present. My grandmother had little to no education and my grandfather, whom I hoped would take her place, had gone out of town on civic duty.
Where was my father?
I had no clue.

Every boy needs a father figure to set him on the path to manhood. how to fix a tie, walk, or speak to a lady. Nicholas Otoo's absence from my life deprived me of unique attributes that created a void within me. I needed him. I had to find him to come by my school to prove to myself and every one of my colleagues that, I too had a father! Grandma Maku had all the answers, and she narrated how he had retired from the Ghana Armed Forces and was working at the American Embassy in Osu. In the company of one of my trusted friends, I set out to look for him at the Embassy. My father existed after all.
"What are you doing here?" The tall, dark man, whom I resembled a lot, asked upon emerging out of the building.
My face dropped.
"My teachers need you to come to my school." I managed to say.
"What wrong have you done? Tell me! If I follow you to that school and I find out you've been naughty, I will call for an assembly and will make sure I discipline you with the cane in my car in front of the whole school."

It was terrifying, but I was also relieved because today, the world would finally know that I had a father. The drive to my school was quiet – a deep silence that sent my mind racing. "What if he gets to discover something I probably did and had forgotten about?" I questioned myself a few times on the road. Rapid flashbacks and racing thoughts kept me static till the ride was over.

I dreaded the walk through the gates of Osu Home School. My father, after pulling out his cane from the trunk of the car, nudged me to lead the way to the headmistress, Mrs Asiedu's office, in what I thought would be a horror show. Mrs Asiedu was a sweet lady who played mum to me sometimes. She was averagely built, had healthy brown skin and would neatly rock her thick black African hair in all manner of styles befitting a headmistress.

"Ah Mr Otoo!" she called.

"Why are you walking behind your son with a cane? He has done nothing wrong"

"Then why have I been summoned here?" He asked arching his brows.

"Please, come have a seat in my office and let's talk."

We walked through the narrow doors of Mrs Asiedu's office and sat in her cushioned visitors' chair. She recounted how I had been nominated to receive an award at the school's speech and prize ceremony and how they needed the presence of a parent to sign a release form for the presentation. His response opened me up to a wider emotional mess. "Hah! Is this why you called me here? To merely sign for an award?" he walked out of the office after pending his signature with disappointment then sucked his teeth to express what he truly made of his unnecessary summon. I wept.

Alas! The day was here and I was adjudged the overall best student. However, my father did not show up to celebrate my accomplishments. Would hate be too strong of a word to use in this case? Well, that's what I felt he emitted towards me.

Sorrow is slow poison to the mind of a child. My pre-teen brain struggled to process the raw event at Mrs Asiedu's office. Did my father not want me? I swept it under the dusty carpet in my mind to create a lump high enough to trip me into a downward spiral. Depression was a word unknown to me but looking back today, I think I had hit that wall unknowingly. That memory took me back to a time before relocating to my grandparents' and enrolling at Osu Home School. This time at Burma Camp Complex placed me on the pathway to unexpected trauma and emotional pain.

My brother and I didn't have a memory of our father. No recollection whatsoever of what he looked like, how he walked, talked or laughed, it was a complete blank. My separated parents lived 10 minutes apart from each other, my father at Burma Camp and the rest of us at 37 Military barracks. However, there were no visitations from our father over the years or an attempt from him to get a glimpse of how his sons fared. Perhaps he didn't care that much, so we held no familiar image of him in our hearts. The man we pictured to be our father was dark, tall and often faceless. On the other hand, he knew exactly what we looked like.

P.T.A meetings were fun days in school. It created avenues for students to take a break from all the long hours of being seated on hard wooden desks, struggling to grasp the concept of whatever topic the teachers effortlessly threw at them. From classroom to classroom we roamed to socialize with other students while the teachers took the opportunity to spill our academic performances and matters arising in the faces of our parents. It was on one such day that I saw my father for the very first time in a flash. We headed towards home from the premises of Burma Camp Complex with our mum in tow and there he was—my father, in the company of a junior colleague, who was my step-sister. Seconds after my mother pointed him out of the multitude outside. he got into his vehicle and drove off, leaving no time for my brother and me to see his face.

4 years in the Burma Camp Complex left me with a shocking discovery that the most important man in my life had been coming to my school every weekday to fetch my step-sister. He drove past us every day like we didn't matter. Left with unanswerable questions, I swept it again under the carpet till the dreaded vis-à-vis at his office at the American embassy. Was it a shame? Some type of disdain? Whatever in this world would cause a father to ignore his offspring?

Perhaps that accounted for my brother's hot temperament. His diminutive stature made him an obvious prey for bullies in school. They pushed him in ways which would mostly trigger a reaction the teachers would not condone. He became rebellious. The bullies enjoyed his bouts of anger as entertainment and before he'd even realise it. He'd be caught in a moment of regret with the school's authorities. I heard screams and shouts during class hours one day. It came from my brother's classroom. Intrigued, the entire Primary 3 class including my teacher, rushed out to the Primary 5 block to satisfy our curiosity. Benjamin, my brother, had climbed onto his class teacher, Mr Asiedu's table and had him by the collar of his shirt. I couldn't believe my eyes. I nearly tripped in a rush to separate them and quizzed Ben on what had occurred. His colleague picked on him in a bid to get a reaction when he did. Mr Asiedu shut him down, held him accountable and pinned the blame on him. He felt misunderstood, unheard and I believe he had had enough of the everyday drama with the bullies, so blinded by the emotional rush, the spectacle we saw ensued.

# Chapter 2

# Chapter 2

I had grown to become my Grandmother's confidant during her latter years in the early 80s. She opened me up to more culinary skills, shared her deepest sentiments and would offer some advice as a compass to navigate the world. Though an average income earner, she had quite a sophisticated taste for the things in life and the few of my Aunties in London at that time showered her with some perfumes and other items from the Queen's city. During one of our private conversations, she walked to one of the bags containing the Britain-imported items and brought out a bottle of Lavender soap and Perfume. She said to me,
"I need you to listen to this instruction carefully, make sure that I am bathed with this soap and perfume on the day of my passing."
"Why?" I asked with concern.
"Just promise me that you will see to it that it is done when the time comes."
I immediately sunk in my spirit but nodded in agreement with an awkward grin on my face.
Wondering in my lost thoughts, I struggled to understand the bizarre instruction. It was the first time she had given a stern directive without her usual stony face. Brooding over that all evening birthed no meaning. As the kid I was, I kicked it aside to make room for a restful night's sleep.

My Grandparents were devout Christians. They both assumed offices at the Epiphany Presbyterian church at Osu Kaajano. My Grandma was part of the women's fellowship and my Grandfather was one of the church leaders. They were not the type to miss Sunday service so once you lived under their roof, it was a requirement to emulate that trait, with this, Ben and I joined the drama team in the Sunday school. The early morning air was filled with good-old Presby hymnals from the radio box in the living room as the aroma of Grandma Maku's corn porridge breakfast filled the air. Both my grandparents were very prayerful. Oblivious to what it entailed or stood for, I made no significant effort to pursue an understanding of it. I knew God created the world we see but that didn't mean I had a relationship with him… "It makes no sense," was an anthem I'd sing to myself whenever discussions or stories about the miraculous works of God would come up.

Sunday afternoons were always fun in South Labadi. Everything a boy needed to have fun was within ten to perhaps twenty blocks on our street. I got to play soccer with my brother and some friends without fear of punishment from Grandma Maku. We would play 'gutter-to-gutter' (local Ghanaian soccer where the poles were positioned with stones and the balls were made of stuffed socks). We would display some incredible skills on the field of play, especially with *'chaskele'* (a local bat-and-ball game). We would make our ball with crushed tin cans and imagine ourselves playing on national television as professionals, it was amazing. However, the reveries were short-lived and there was always the harsh reality of awakening back into real life where we were not even halfway to being pros. We got our chores done early to watch the *Osofo Dadzie* television series at 8 pm which was a big deal in the 80s. It was an authentic Ghanaian production which told a variety of stories by re-enacting true-life issues with a pinch of comedy. This local dramedy troupe led by S.K Oppong also starred legends like Bea Kissi, super OD, Frimpong Manso and Fred Addai among others and it was simply not to be missed! Osofo Dadzie's plays always had the right doses of bliss and lessons to crown the weekend and welcome in a new week.

Television on Monday evenings was not so thrilling. The only thing to look forward to was the 'Talking Point' show and as the name suggests, all they did was talk for unending hours about national and social issues. What's a platter of current affairs to an eleven-year-old? My grandfather was an ardent fan. He would stay glued to our black and white television set and yell out a comment or two at the guests on the show, almost as if they could hear him. He played the role of "the invisible panellist" to perfection.

I believe I was almost turning thirteen when my mum began settling back home at 37 Military Barracks. The army placed her on fewer external assignments so Ben and I could finally go back home to be with her. It was coincidentally around the same time Grandma Maku's health was deteriorating. It was bad enough that I was leaving my confidant but seeing her in a constant state of fragility broke my heart. Ben and I came up with an idea to pay her visits every day after school so she wouldn't miss too much of us. In our mum's military flat, the table of the favourites had turned in my favour. I was inarguably the favourite at my mum's. Ben detested that fact, while at my grandparents, Ben was the chosen one--at least that's what we both thought. He was quick to blame it all on his disability which to me had gotten stale at that point. This created some sort of rivalry which stayed with us for quite a long time. Of course, I denied being the culprit whenever I created a stir or caused any form of mischief. My brother would eye me with disgust as he boldly confessed to being behind the acts. I knew he'd always return with a knife ready to fight me after bearing my cross so I always geared up for those altercations. Oooooh, the memories! My mother tells a story of the afternoon of May 15th 1979 less than five weeks before the national elections. It was the day of the attempted coup d'état in Ghana. It was a Tuesday morning when our mother sent us to school. I was at the time enrolled at Burma Camp kindergarten. This was years before moving in with Grandma Maku. After dropping us off at school, she departed for Makola market in a commercial bus locally known as *'tro-tro'* after a few hours to shop for some groceries. On her return, she noticed the 37 Military roads were quieter than usual. All other vehicles she saw were rushing and so were the people in the streets. She describes feeling as though she were cast in a movie about the apocalypse. It was quite an unusual thing to see a major street in Accra that empty. She arrived safely at her quarters still unsure of what had occurred. As she unloaded her shopping bag, there came a startling knock on the door. An army officer had brought her two boys home. "What's the problem Sah?" She inquired with concern. The soldier proceeded to scold her for leaving her kids to roam freely in the streets at a time of national insecurity. "I had no clue Sah. I assumed they were still in school." she had no idea we had been sent home from school earlier to be with our families because of the coup. Intrigued by the dispatch of military armour cars and soldiers shooting on the streets, my brother and I at that tender age, saw it as a great time to fetch our toy guns to join the soldiers in fighting for the nation. We were barrack boys after all, and to us, it implied a need to perform our duties with the military and follow what the soldiers showcased on the streets of 37 El-Wak stadium roads. *Pow! Pow! Pow!* We mimicked with our lips, the sounds of the many gunshots we heard on the streets with glee while aiming the toy guns at each other. The naivety and innocence! Fortunately, we got grabbed in the middle of our guise by the serving officer who brought us safely home to our mother before the country's state of security became dire. In light of this, my mother had us transported in a military vehicle to south Labadi temporarily for two weeks. It was the longest we had been away from her at the time. As the head of the emergency unit at the military hospital, she was a front-line worker in the chaos of the coup busily picking up and treating the injured in the ambulance. It was all everyone talked about, the coup. It was all over the news. Ma had to wait to be sure there was an order before coming to fetch us from our family house. My brother and I shared in the silliest of imaginations and embarked on the craziest of adventures as we grew, yet our unending rivalry stayed with us till a dark December–the month which would change the trajectory of our lives together as a family.

**It was a day in 1985.** Unsure of what to do that day after school that fateful day, a sudden urge to visit my ailing Grandma swept through my mind. There was often not much left to do after school, especially during examination week. Still wandering on the school's compound, it dawned on me again to see Granny. It was almost like there was a higher power calling out loud to me to see her. Heeding the voice, I carefully scrutinized all zippers and pockets on my backpack and shorts with hopes of finding some change to get on board a *tro-tro* from Burma Camp to South Labadi but who was I kidding? Looking back, it's safe to say that it was merely a desperate act of faith. The walk to South Labadi Estates was a long one. The distraction on the road was good company. The petty quarrels among *tro-tro* drivers continuously honking loudly amidst hurling out vulgar words in a blend of *Twi and Ga* (local Ghanaian dialects) at the traffic lights and the competition between the athletic street hawkers running in-between traffic lanes under the scorching sun to get their *Insu* (sachet water) to the bus passengers sticking their arms out the bus window to snatch the delivery. My body, in an attempt to cool itself from the heat wave, created beads of sweat which freely run down my temples to the collar of my shirt. Then came that gut feeling again…something felt off.

Loud wails and screams from my grandparents' house attracted

neighbours and passersby. From five blocks away, I could hear the distinguishing voice of Aunty Ruby Abadji calling out to me. "Joojo, what are you doing here? You aren't supposed to be here."
She asked.
"Go, please go to your mum's place. I will come to fetch you later."
It was an obvious attempt to hinder me from going any further.
"I'm here to see Grandma Maku. Is she home?" I quizzed.
It was the first time I had seen Aunt Ruby speechless. We stood in stiffening silence for a split second before the neighbours urged her to give me access to my grandparents' house. Her face dropped as the feigned smile on her face faded away. Then it hit me, Maku had gone to be with the Lord. Blinded by tears, I walked into the compound with all the courage I could muster and Aunty Ruby behind. Recalling the final wish of Grandma, I led the elders of the house to the inner room to retrieve the lavender soap and perfume she had instructed to ensure she was bathed with upon her demise. All she had previously instructed some few years ago suddenly had meaning. Her death awakened in me an urgency to be better, to do more and be different. The heartbreak was indescribable. Picking up the pieces after losing a loved one hurts. The blow was a difficult one to recover from especially for my Grandfather who had spent his entire adult life loving this woman who had become the essence of his being. Laying down her casket 6 feet beneath the ground brought the realization that he had indeed lost the love of his life. It's all coming back to me now. It was December 5th 1985.

**1985/86** reeled in a pile of pain. Six months after laying Grandma Maku to rest, My Grandfather, Mr. Gilbert Baah Abadji also passed away. Right at the point where we had come to terms with Grandma's demise and had laid down our load of misery, Grandpa bade us farewell. It was as if my family had been placed in an endless slide of anguish. My Grandfather, I have come to believe could no longer bear the absence of his late wife. He had silently walked down the lonely road of grief till he gave up the ghost on July 2nd 1986. Felt like the wound in our hearts was being pricked by a dagger. From that point, I had come to a personal conclusion that the Universe was deliberately working against us. We were in Shambles. We had lost the founts of the family and had no clue where to go from there. Water turned sour, food was bland and nothing made sense.

As the ambitious boy, I had concluded on my High School options before taking the finals. Presbyterian Boys Secondary School (PRESEC) was a personal first choice with Mawuli Secondary School as the second. I imagined a problem-free future by becoming an *"Odadi*j*"* (a title for PRESEC alumni), walking through those gates, I dreamt, would certainly usher me into greatness. Money is not everything they say, but the absence of it certainly stifled my dreams of becoming an *Odadi*j. My mother had more than enough on her plate to tackle. from our medical expenses, food, clothing, utility bills etc in addition to catering for herself. An apparent way to alleviate her struggles of raising funds for our Secondary education was to opt for a school she could afford. At some point, I did not want to go to secondary school at all, for me, it was PRESEC or nothing. Every military officer is entitled to a handsome discount in fees among other academic expenses for their wards in all Military schools, hence settling to be a freshman in Burma Camp Secondary school (BUCASS) in 1985, was a sure way of saying, *"I see your pain. I understand that you have to do everything on your own. I love you enough to put your needs before mine."* However, that did not erase the hurt of seeing other colleagues enrolled at the schools of their choice with utmost joy while I had to embrace the idea of becoming a day student at BUCASS as a compromise. Poverty surely ate away my dream with no crumbs left behind. Along the line, I would learn that a school's popularity was not a determinant factor in one's future— it was all about you and the zeal to make it.

To add to the injury, my cousins, Nene and Darley were enrolled in good schools. Nene was a Presecan in my dream school while Darley attended one of the best all-girls schools in Ghana, Aburi Girls Secondary School. Their life in comparison to ours was a complete irony. These cousins were flown to London almost every vacation to get rid of pent-up academic stress. Yeah, they enjoyed the 'soft life' from scratch. Whenever they'd invite Ben and me to come over for a visit upon arrival, we would try in every way possible to sit it out. Don't get me wrong. To be thrown an invitation felt great, to fit in with the hosts on the other hand was the issue. Our financial woes and underprivileged societal status were enough discouragement to keep us from showing up at our cousins'. Their "hand-me-downs" were the new apparel my brother and I wore with pride every day, hence the notion of not belonging with them. Those were certainly unpleasant times.

Secondary School marked a whole new chapter in my life. New friends, a whole new adventure of bagging a GCA O' Level on a new campus with other barracks boys and girls with Ben. While some students were welcoming, others were simply unpleasant. Surprised? Well, let me describe a typical day for a secondary school "fresher" in Ghana. A walk through the halls of terror made you prey to merciless seniors who had 'mean' embedded in their DNA. All freshmen are assembled and coerced to perform all manner of humiliating acts to entertain the seniors— they called us *"homodwan"* (fresh breed). It was a required ritual for all freshmen to undergo. Something was displeasing about some of the kids born to military parents in our school. They were brutally mean and big bullies. It was a struggle to make it through the halls of BUCASS daily without any of these kids getting on my last nerves. It was no paradise for Ben as his disability once again became a centre of attraction for hungry predators who were seeking a day of unlimited laughter and entertainment. As with anything, though, you learn to adapt. Secondary School gave me a feigned sense of maturity and a taste of freedom which cajoled me into becoming overly acquainted with ill-mannered students. During class hours, we would make our way out of the school to organize some fun for ourselves at a colleague's house. We would play some music, eat some food and sip any beverage we would lay our hands on. Would it have killed us to wait until recess to indulge? Of course not! Guess we deceived ourselves into believing that, we had a point to prove to ourselves that we too were "sharp guys." On a day luck eluded us, we were caught and placed in a Military guard room and disciplined very well by Military officers to serve as a deterrent to others — it was a turning point for me. I was able to turn over a new leaf and do away with the ugliness I had ignorantly adopted. Other barrack boys who still saw a need to keep the act going were apprehended and expelled.

The Prodigal son had found his way back onto the course he had veered off. The highs on the detour were short-lived as the transformed me paid more attention to all lessons in my new Home Science Class. You read that right! I read Home science as an elective in secondary school. Initially, we were all made to study similar subjects till it was time to opt for our individual courses. I passed most of the time pondering over various courses and what to do with my stay at BUCASS. Trickles of conversations going on among the students with debates mostly

centred on which classes embodied more fun rather than which would play a vital role in shaping one's future. Their laughter and giggles played a perfect background to my pensive mood. I was a long way from finding my purpose, I thought. The dream of becoming a doctor still lingered. Registering as a Biology student would be the closest to realizing that dream, still putting my mum's needs before mine, I wondered how she would afford to foot the bills of the seemingly endless years of attaining a doctorate. Choosing Biology, to me would be a dead end. My late Grandma had sown in me a passion for cooking which my mother adored, with that seed I was encouraged to take up Home Science as a major. The tone of mockery in the condescending manner with which I was addressed by my peers was discouraging.
"Francis, Catering is for women o! Do you now identify as one?" They would often ask amid laughter.

They were supportive of everyone else except for me. The idea of seeing a male in a "feminine" class was an invitation for jests and mockery. To worsen my woes, I found myself as the only male in a class of thirty females. Whenever it was time for catering practicals, we would carry our baskets containing all the necessary equipment and ingredients required for the cooking lesson of the day. My friends would line up as we walked by and yell, *"Kwadwo besia"* which translates to an effeminate man. I would dread going back to school on subsequent days knowing perfectly well what awaited me in the halls of BUCASS.

Days of hardships persisted. The normalcy of hawking petty items on the streets to support our upkeep kept me away from school for some days. I had finally been set on a path I was passionate about yet, the lack of finances had become a canker. Ben still hooked on his childhood dream, left BUCASS for

Nungua Secondary Technical with hopes of becoming a technician. As you may have guessed, his stature again, subjected him to bullies of all kinds. Unable to stomach it this time, he stayed away from school too many times and got himself expelled. Feelings of unworthiness began creeping into his mind, ultimately, he felt unloved and not human enough. His disability had in a way become his curse. He became acquainted with pain and would often shy away from the company of others.

"Nobody likes me." I caught him saying that a few times to himself.
How could I not? He was my brother after all... I loved him dearly. It became difficult for him to get closer to anyone regardless of how much he forced himself to. All he knew was fear, depression had laid its ugly paws on my brother. He believed whatever it told him. He had regurgitated the continuous thrums of *"nobody likes you"* in his mind for so long that it had become the gospel he knew. My mother reached out to help and so did the rest of the family. He eventually became indulged in alcoholism which deteriorated his health.

# Chapter 3

# Chapter 3

My mother's heart ached. It did from over-exerting herself in a bid to seek help for Ben. He had moved to Takoradi barracks with my mum in 2004 when she was transferred by her superiors. Often left with nothing to do at home himself, he proceeded to fraternize with soldiers at the "other ranks" section of the barracks. She wanted badly for Kwesi to be useful. In the '90s, while the legendary Ghanaian actress Grace Omaboe aka Maame Dokono and Dr Rokoto starred in the children's educational programme, 'By the fireside', which was centred on the exploits of Kweku Ananse, My mother thought it a great idea to have Kwesi enrolled with the Performing Arts troupe. At the time, He had been expelled from Nungua Secondary Technical School, so all he had was ample time on his hands to be productive in other ways. Kwesi expressed his feelings most succinctly after rounds of discussions. He was uninterested.

Ma liked to pray. She prayed a lot over us and more for Kwesi. She prayed over us while we comfortably slept on our yellow porous mattress. I caught her a few times with one eye open. She sat at the edge of the bed I shared with my brother in her home at the Military barracks. She made a sign of the cross on our foreheads with anointing oil. She also prayed in a strange language, they call it tongues speaking.

*"Make my children great oh Lord! Keep their feet on the path that you have marked for them. Let not their enemies rejoice over them in any way oh Lord! May all who see them celebrate my*

*God. Give them the courage to follow the life that you have called them to."*

I had memorized these lines because she prayed for them a lot. Mama tended to switch up every morning. When we woke up from our sleep, she'd yell wildly at us at any simple blunder we committed as if she hadn't cried over us in prayer the night before. For all the times we lived with Ma, she never missed a night of praying over us. The love of a mother…au naturel yet inexplicable. Ma liked to sing too; Every Sunday morning, while we got ready for church, every time she cleaned the front porch or dusted the cushioned sofa in the living room. The funny thing was when we misbehaved; she was quick to put her worship songs on hold to give us the scolding of a lifetime. After concluding her many words with a simple *'Ah'*, she'd slide smoothly back into worship, as if nothing happened. Ma was such a character, like Grandma Maku.

Anyway, fast forward to Takoradi in 2004, my mother began noticing some items missing from her mini deep freezer. Perhaps she thought it was the forgetfulness of old age setting in but it wasn't the case. She was baffled by the concept of items magically leaving a house she only occupied with Ben with no other party coming in or out. She confided in Maghajia her neighbour, about the mysterious disappearances of her items. "Ah *hw*j so you haven't heard *erh*?" Maghajia replied. "ȷ*nj*e let me tell you, Whenever you take off to work, Ben carries your stuff to give to some ladies at the main bar at the other ranks side in exchange for some *akpeteshie* dry gin." Mama was ashamed. She thought Ben had called it quits with that lifestyle before moving to Takoradi. She greeted him with a stoic face as he walked through the doors of the simple living room. He knew she was aware of what he had done yet he acted as though nothing had occurred. Mama mentioned the backyard poultry she started in the cheaply crafted coop she had some carpenters design. She would normally walk into Ben's room to fetch his laundry from his drawers on weekends as he slept. As she pulled the drawers open one Saturday, a dozen eggs came rolling forward. Aggravated she called, "Kwesi, Kwesi, are fowls laying in your drawers now?" He replied, "ooooh Ma! Please don't bother me with this." "No need to get violent, young man! Just explain to me how the eggs got in here?" He murmured and shrugged as he walked out on her. Theirs was a rocky relationship till she was sent to Liberia on a peacekeeping mission in December of 2004. Worried about leaving Ben by himself with his new hobby, she sent him packing to Uncle Seth's residence at Odorkor in Accra. Though Ben and Uncle Seth weren't on the very best speaking terms at the time, my mother simply had no choice. It was days to her final departure to Liberia when she decided to visit her brother and also check in on her son but was met with a rather aggravating scene. Uncle Seth had beaten up Ben mercilessly. Beyond displeased yet keeping her cool, she questioned her brother on the reason behind his actions. He narrated how Ben had taken out some of his possessions in exchange for alcohol like he did with her at Takoradi. Shame befell her. She could barely look her brother in the eye. "Jesus, take the wheel," was all she could whisper to herself as she left the scene downcast. We weren't sure about what drew Kwesi into alcoholism. Was it a fascination with the trickle of the hot pungent gin down his throat or how his appetite grew with every gulp of the chilled sweaty bottles of beer?

Mama's nightmares started the moment she left for Liberia. One night she dreamt of Kwesi being thrown alive into a dark pit. As he lay below struggling to move his body, the people gathered around the pit began covering him with sand. Mama lay rigid in bed as she tried to free herself from the weight that seemed to have pinned her down on her mattress. It was terrifying. She finally broke free and awoke with palpitations and tremors. Was her son okay? She called home the next morning to see how Kwesi was faring. "He's okay. He stepped out a moment ago. Would you like to speak to him?" Uncle Seth asked. "No, it's fine. I just had the strangest dream that's all." "That's all? *Daabi* sister, tell me what you saw in that dream." "I saw Kwesi being buried in a pit by faceless people and…" "And what, sister? *Erh*" Uncle Seth cut in. "You should not be paying attention to these silly things." She held back her thoughts and said her goodbyes. However, her pastor was receptive to the spiritual indications of the bizarre dream and prayed with her over the phone. She remembers readying her luggage filled with Liberian goodies for our cousins, her siblings and of course Kwesi, a few days after her arrival in Takoradi on June 27th, 2005.

Without prior notice, one of my uncles in Prestea had sent a taxi driver to fetch my mother immediately to the State Transport Corporation to board the next available bus to Accra. It was the morning of July 2nd, 2005 and Uncle Seth had called for an emergency meeting at his Odorkor Residence which specially required my mother's presence. Mama was highly principled. she despised any agenda with impromptu embedded on it. The driver nearly turned to the car when Mama loudly communicated over the phone to her brother about her displeasure. 30 minutes went by before she agreed to go with the driver to the station. There was a slight pause before the driver asked in a low tone, "Ma, should I start the car?" He certainly did not wish to aggravate the issue any further. As they exited the barracks, her phone rang. It was a niece she hadn't heard from in quite a while.

*"Eii,* how are you my dear?" she greeted with joy. "We haven't spoken in a while.
"Yes oo Ma, I'm well. Have you heard what has happened?"
"No ooo my dear. What has happened?"
*"Ah!* So you mean no one has informed you?" she added.
She retorted, "Hey my dear, why are you dancing around whatever information you're withholding? I have been summoned to Accra this morning without notice and I am in no mood for guess games."
"Hmm. Sorry to inform you Ma. Kwesi is dead."
Ma went numb. She could hear her heartbeat in her ears. Her feet were cold and her eyes widened with shock. This could not be happening. The Taxi driver observed her demeanour through the rearview mirror and asked if he should drive her back home. "No please take me to the station. I need to get to Accra in the exact state I'm in," she replied. "Go with God," the driver said with sympathy as he helped Ma load her luggage onto the bus. Still trying to wrap her mind around the validity of the devastating news she had received, her phone rang again, this time it was one of her younger brothers in London. He asked, "Sister how are you?" with a deepening sense of concern. He had called because the news of Ben's demise had reached the other half of the family in the Diaspora.
"I'm fine"
"Sister, I said how are you?"
She rolled her eyes in exasperation, "Ah Bra, I said I'm fine." She retorted sitting side by side with other nosy passengers on board the STC bus. It would be wrong to let her ravaged emotions get the best of her. She gracefully exercised every bit of patience left in her
"Are you sure you are okay?" he probed further.
*"Hoh*! Stop spewing nonsense, if you have nothing better to say to me, to hell with you." Her eyes caught other passengers who

nearly twisted their necks as they turned to look away from her. Ma could care less what run through their minds. she's a woman who just lost a son, the very one who ushered her into motherhood for the first time. She would be calm, she thought in silence. She would be her regular courteous self when she got to Odorkor to discuss the death of her son.

The nanny who took care of her sister's kids was a sweet old lady. She often greeted Ma with a fixated broad smile followed by endless conversations which covered a chain of topics ranging from domestic to political issues which Ma found amusing. Sadly, she didn't care much for it that day. She chose the seat facing the exit, with that, she could stare blankly into the streaming sun rays from the trap door and drown out all other voices when conversations got real. If only she hadn't left for Liberia, Kwesi would have been alive. Maybe, he would have waited to set eyes on his mother before giving up the ghost. Perhaps, she should have been a little more lenient with him. Kwesi's demise made Ma feel guilty, mostly for being unavailable to her son in his final moments.

Uncle Seth walked in after an hour to join the rest of the family at the sitting. "Vic is that you?" He asked with the intent of breaking the awkward silence.
"Yes it is, who else could it be?"
"Have you been offered some water?"
"Yes I have."
"Good, good. But I hope you performed a little libation before taking a sip."
"Seth *paaa*, I've never seen our parents or any other member of this family offer libation to the gods before having a drink of any kind. I'm sorry I can't." Ma was determined not to be put down or be patronized in the moment. Uncle Seth gave a shrug as he

exited with a cup of water in hand to offer his libation to appease the gods before consuming the rest in a big gulp. They all sat in a bowl of mixed emotions as everyone waited on the other to formally break the news. Eyes rolled from side to side, exchanging glances as a means to silently communicate the question of *who to break the news?*.

The neighbourhood had organised a series of funerals that week and to Kwesi, it was a call to a drinking spree. Carefully, he slid through several funeral gatherings to consume all he could drink and more. Intoxicated by a variety of concoctions, he could barely find his balance as he moved in a rhythmic sway towards the next funeral tent for a few more free bottles. By the end of the evening, he was carried to the gate of the house by some sympathizers who thought he had ridiculed himself enough. Ben had fortunately regained consciousness later that night and crawled his way indoors. Everyone had left the house by the time Ben awoke the next morning. At Odorkor, Waste car operators rode through the neighbourhood on early mornings during weekends to collect domestic waste from all households at a fee. Realizing it was almost time for their vehicle to pull up on their street, Ben called an aunt for some money to settle the collectors. Though he placed the call three times for the fee, he was completely ignored. Perhaps, they were under the impression that Kwesi would use the cash to serve a different purpose. It was unusual for him to not come out of his room. He spent most hours of the day out with his buddies and would only come home for meals. Several hours passed, yet the nanny had neither heard his voice nor the sound of banging doors to signify his presence at home. Troubled, she walked into his room only to find him semi-conscious on the floor. He had a temperature and struggled to say a word. He was immediately rushed to the Labadi Polyclinic where he was diagnosed with Body Integrity disorder (BID) and

Pneumonia. Upon realizing how critical his condition was, the doctors approved an immediate transfer to the Korle Bu Teaching Hospital.

Ma sipped her water slowly, "why Korle Bu?" she asked in confusion. "Why was he not transferred to 37 Military Hospital where he would have received priority care?" They assumed her being away in Liberia would deprive him of any sort of special care at 37. Exchanging words with the rest of the family in the middle of narration would be useless. It wasn't going to bring Kwesi back to life. He was gone and that was all there was to it. When Uncle Seth called to inform my father about the demise of his first son, he didn't seem all perturbed about the news. *"Well, let me know when you're settled on the final date for the burial. I'll be there,"* was all he could say in acknowledgement. There were days Ma would wake up from her sleep and everything looked fuzzy. She could hear the voice of Kwesi almost calling out to her. All the times they had argued over the most trivial things kept coming back to her. She had missed him. My uncles and other relatives barred her from entering the morgue on the day of the post-mortem. She was restrained outside the premises to only receive the body of her son to 37 Military Hospital for storage to await burial. On the other hand, I had only spoken to my brother 3 days before his death. I was out of the country on a job opportunity. we had patched up our differences and talked about reconnecting and having a good time in December of 2005. This memory still cuts deeper than a knife yet, knowing we had made amends gives me a little satisfaction. He died knowing that he was loved dearly... by me.

Kwesi's alcoholism was disturbing to the family. It created a certain personality they were not accustomed to. They intervened with good intentions but he made them disappear with a cast of an invisible spell. Depression is a mind-eating disease which slowly devours your self-worth and eventually your sanity. Let's be cautious of what we pay attention to.

Meanwhile, in BUCASS, absence from school attracted piles of punishments including weeding on the vast school field coupled with receiving a number of lashes on my buttocks which I was always well prepared for. I had excellent weeding skills which made it less of a hefty task to execute at a point, for the whippings I would put on thick layers of shorts as a shield to cushion my buttocks. Being abreast with the forms of punishment to look out for making it easy to miss out on school — this time for a good cause. Prior to any exam, I would borrow notes and textbooks from colleagues as means to catch up with all lessons missed. On some days, when school was over, I would stay back at the assembly hall or snuggle myself into a cubicle after 'Taekwondo' practice with the borrowed books to grasp as much as I could before the owners came badgering for them. It was dizzying. Gifted with a rare photographic memory enhanced my ability to score high marks in English Language, Agricultural Science, and Environmental Studies. Those were a piece of cake! Well, except for Mathematics which I found a little too complicated for my liking. Sir Ablazo, the Math teacher, upon noticing my struggling performance with the subject, encouraged me to follow all laid down systematic approaches to solving various math questions with the same zeal I pursued other subjects. It wasn't all rainbows in the end but I did score a little beyond average. 'Ablazo' was his moniker throughout our stay in school. it makes it quite difficult to recall what his actual name really was.

Nonetheless, my teachers loved me. During lessons I took

pleasure in throwing unanswerable questions at them, followed by the "hows" and "whys" as the other students murmured in the background in a bid to silence me. Undeterred, I'd go as far as ushering myself into the Staff common room in a bid to seek further elaborations to my follow-up questions. My curiosity became a nuisance they initially sought to avoid. However, they gravitated more towards me and furnished me with the necessary directives to fully comprehend whatever I found mind-boggling. The finals were here! I was learning all the time now. It was my responsibility to excel and make mama proud. This was a "make it or break it" period for me— I could not afford to fail to retake it all at another time. Students were flaming out to libraries, study halls, and extra class appointments all with a common goal of passing the finals. For me, it implied more late night studies, more copying and comparing notes with others, more alone times at the assembly hall and even more early morning studies. There was no time to be seduced by play or gossip. This was war. With the aid of a printed exam schedule timetable o the School's notice board, we were able to determine which days to put in the extra work. I had confidence in facing all other subjects with confidence except for Math; it was like having a final face-off with a big bully. Gladly, Sir Ablazo's counsel on the tactical approach to math eased me off a bit. The entire exam period was roughly three weeks and we had six months to await the results. Six months of my uncertainty, Six months of swimming in a pool of doubt, "What if I failed?" "What if I'm floored by a particular subject?" These were among the many questions I'd ask myself. The waiting period was also a time to look into tertiary schools. I had high hopes of taking my newfound passion for catering a step further. My mind was deliberately planting seeds of success before it even came. When it came to my culinary skills, my mum was the number one cheerleader. It initially seemed like she was throwing her weight behind me because I seemed highly capable of taking over from her in the kitchen but that was far from the case. She had foreseen a future for her little boy in catering and did everything she could to get me to see the bigger picture despite our hardships. With her encouragement, I accepted the challenge and intensified the search for a tertiary school big enough to accommodate my purpose. Fortunately, she had a colleague who was connected to someone at Ho Technical who I heard at the time, was the best school offering catering tuition in Ghana hence. Gaining entry became my topmost priority. On the other hand, admissions for catering students were closed that year, so the deal we agreed on was to stay in the engineering class for a year and be re-admitted into the Culinary Arts class the subsequent year. I finally had faith in the story of my life.

News on the release of our Examination results spread across like wildfire. I rushed to the premises of the BUCASS to see what fate had in store for me. A part of me knew I would make the cut while the rest of me still wallowed in doubts. Mixed expressions on the faces of students gathered by the notice board made my stomach turn. With a brave face, I turned to the notice board to see my name among the first five students to emerge with distinction. I was beyond relieved. Our headmistress did not hesitate to express her pride in us. The joy that rushed through my body was inexplicable. To become the only student in the Home Science class to graduate with distinction in the class of **1988** was a cape I would wear all my life. All worries I had been harbouring about my future seemed to slowly fall away with this feat because to me, I had already half departed to my dream school.

# Chapter 4

# Chapter 4

Ho Technical, later Ho Polytechnic, presently Ho Technical University is situated in the heart of Ho, the capital of the Volta Region of Ghana. Before modernization set in, Ho Technical wasn't your regular fancy-looking school with tall buildings standing in every corner. There were mostly simple scattered buildings on a vast land within a green forest-like area which created an aesthetically pleasing to the eye coupled with an atmosphere conducive for learning. This was before the eruption of banks, ATMs and gigantic structures we presently see across tertiary schools in Ghana. Accra with its usual hustle and bustle, noise and air pollution could not compare to the serenity I enjoyed in Ho. The air was clean. Uncle Seth Abadji, the eldest of my mother's siblings, in one way or the other played a role of a financier at some point in my education. He was a football enthusiast and the former chairman of Accra Hearts of Oak Football Club. He served the Great Phobia with the late president, H.E John Evans Atta Mills as his vice chair. Uncle Seth was a well-to-do man at the time who contributed his quota to my education when the need arose. He made available to me all kinds of provisions for my feeding and upkeep in Ho Technical. Before the much-awaited departure to Ho, I visited my best buddy. Aunty Ruby met me with a welcoming smile and a greeting in Ga I had gotten used to, "Joojo, you are here. Oh, come inside. It's been a while." This was always followed by a series of questions enquiring of her sister and my brother." This manner of greeting is still the order of the day in every typical Ghanaian extended family home. I found it refreshing. It was her

way of expressing her utmost love and concern towards us.
"I'm informed of your entry into Ho Technical. I'm very proud of you." She continued in Ga.
"Thank you"
"When are you to report?"
"In a few days. I should have reported a while ago but you already know how tough times have gotten."
"Yes, I know. Please listen to me Joojo. You are moving out into the world to begin the first steps towards a career. Your family will not be there with you. You will be exposed to people from various backgrounds and upbringings so before you get overly acquainted ad carried away by their lifestyles, take a minute to remember where you are coming from. Remember, the kind of family that raised you and act accordingly."

I was dumbfounded. Judging by her demeanour, I could feel her counsel truly came from a good place. Her words stuck with me.

I began the four-hour journey by road from Accra to Ho through Sogakope in the final trimester of 1988 to a new beginning, which would become the firm fount upon which my career would be built. We arrived at Adaklu –Anyigbe, one of the eighteen districts in the Volta Region and home to the spectacular Adaklu Mountain. The mountain sat 12km away from Ho and was idolised by the local Ewe inhabitants of Adaklu-Anyigbe. It looked almost life-like. Its breathtaking view instantly shifted my mood, felt like God's way of telling me to be present at that moment and behold His beauty. I felt a cocktail of emotions. the joy of setting my dreams in motion, fear of the uncertainties awaiting me plus the concern surrounding leaving my mother behind. Aunty Ruby was right, it was embarking on this new journey alone… my family meant the world to me and I dared not to disappoint them, though my heart was heavy, crying was not an option. Like they say in Akan, "*Berima ensu*," meaning, "a man does not cry." I stomached the pain and shoved down the emotions to reveal the face of a brave young man excited about his new school.

ADMISSION GRANTED, COURSE OF CHOICE DENIED! I had gained entry into my preferred school, yet, was placed in an engineering class against my will, I had to figure out how to work with wood and create items with metal. By the power vested in me, I declared this new love affair doomed to fail from the start. Surprisingly, with zero effort and interest, I somehow topped the engineering class that year. Catering had already been embedded in my DNA and if it meant repeating an entire year to gain entry into the culinary arts class I'd do so without batting an eye.

Emerging at the top of a "masculine" class I had wanted nothing to do with, encouraged members of the school's administration to coerce me into staying with the other engineering students for the subsequent year. Why? I asked. The agreement was to repeat a whole year of school in order to be registered with the catering class. I remember getting defensive. They thought my mother would be the best to cajole me into agreeing with their demands. She recalls hearing a loud yell as she walked through the gates of Ho Tech, *"I want to do catering, why on earth are you trying to get me to stay with the engineering class? I won't."* It was quite obvious that my mum was taken aback by the scene. She knew the little boy she raised would never cower from a fight but she least expected that I would go off on the administrators in the manner I did. When push comes to shove, the flames of true passion can be blinding when its path is hindered. Perhaps I thought that if I had been denied every good thing in life till this point, I was not going to allow the very thing that gave me a sense of purpose to be taken away from me. My mum walked into the inner office to plead with the officers to have her son stay in his class of choice to let sleeping dogs lie. She knew if the issue was left unresolved, she could not afford to be travelling to Ho every week till I was settled. It was the longest I had ever had to wait at the administration block for the final verdict. After what seemed like forever, they finally agreed to give me entry into the catering class.

I sat again as a first-year student in Ho Tech as a Culinary Arts student. My display of impeccable skills quickly drew a lot of people to me. Slowly and willingly, I warmed and opened myself up to the rest of the class. Not to brag, but I performed better than the ladies in the class. As they leaned in for guidance on class lessons, I cooked up a way to make something out of it. "How about barter?" I quizzed one of the ladies. "I'll only help with theory lessons if you'll agree to share your provisions with me." She reluctantly consented. My new trade landed me a bunch of friends, some of whom held the candle to light up my path while others nearly dragged me into a great deal of destruction. Survival on campus to me was by any means necessary. To be enrolled in the Culinary Arts class was no joke, it involved spending a lot of money on the numerous practicals we had per semester. As a military officer, my mother was entitled to soft loans from the pay office at the barracks. With this, she supported me in the smallest ways she could. Nevertheless, she failed to mention her many trips to the pay office to borrow more money to contribute to my culinary studies. Her first trip to the pay office was after my Grandfather passed away. Her siblings had invited her to a gathering to hold discussions on raising funds for the funeral. With almost nothing to her name, she fell on the pay office for some to present to her siblings as her quota towards the proceedings. Vic had a long list of items to purchase concerning the funeral as well, to beat time. She made her way to Makola to make her bulk purchases. Swarmed by the linear chain of stalls selling almost the same commodities, she finally found one that sold everything on her list. Enquiries were in motion, bargains were struck and purchases were finally made after almost an hour, all she had left to do was to make cash payment. "Ah *Awurade*, my purse is gone!" she yelled after searching her bag thoroughly, "Oh Auntie, I had gone to borrow some money. God, the money is gone." It was quite humiliating as she exited the market square lost in thoughts with a blank facial expression which could be likened to a zombie. It took some passersby and the loud honks from the *tro-tro* drivers to startle her as she had already walked right into the main road without realising it. Touched by her plight, someone offered to lend her some money to complete what she had started. There she was, accruing double debts in a day through no fault of hers.

Yam croquettes–now that's a treat! Seasoned mashed yam fused with butter, bread crumbs, minced fish and an extra mix of simple spices placed me among the top in class. It was the very first food practical in the Culinary Arts Class. Definitely better than figuring out how to make hinges and squares in the confines of a class I was not in tune with. Within a given estimated time, all students were to prepare these croquettes among other treats I, unfortunately, can't recall. I mean not to sing my praise, but I delivered the task to perfection in less than the given duration. Together with about six other students, we were adjudged the best.

In 1990, between my second and third year at Ho Poly, I registered with City and Guilds to read a UK-corresponding catering course in Ghana. The institution, founded originally in the United Kingdom, had several branches in Africa which focused on credentialing skills focused on the future needs of individuals and organisations alike. Mrs Matekpor was among the few teachers at Ho Poly who had taken a liking to me. I remember the affection in her eyes masked with a little seriousness whenever she assisted with preparations for the exam. I never understood why she believed in my passion, perhaps she was a chosen light worker on my journey who executed her assignment with all the love she could. Mrs Matekpor would go out of her way to organise one-on-one lesson sessions with me at any available given time to help out with the study materials. A year later, I passed the Food and Beverage Part I Exam and emerged with excellence among 20 students.

Among those who took an immediate liking to me was a senior who bore the same surname as me, Otoo. As a father would, Otoo gave necessary advice and began looking out for me right from my first to the third year. I did take provisions to school, but they were only enough to fend for myself to a point... that's where Senior Otoo's support came in handy. As a young man with an overwhelming number of wants, there were some things I would not ask my family to provide. Even if I could, I knew my mum could not afford the luxury of going on a splurge for my wants. My primary concern was about her well-being and peace of mind. Senior Otoo supported my upkeep in school in these areas and ensured I was content at the end of each day. Despite his immense contribution throughout my stay in school, my poor memory fails to capture the name of Senior Otoo, the Man who held me down in Ho Tech in full. The biggest blow came when the time came for him to leave campus. it implied finding other means to fend for myself. I thought, "Things would have been much easier if my father was actively involved in my upbringing, Struggling would have been a stranger to me." But wishes aren't horses, are they? As times progressed, I got acquainted with a colleague whose family owned and operated one of the leading laundry companies with some branches in Ghana at the time, Wise Way Cleaners. Patricia Biney as I knew her would often allocate a portion of her provisions to me. at the end of every semester, she would allow me to get on board their Accra-bound private vehicle and invited me over to their home on school re-openings as her mother, Madam Bernice Akua Asabea Azah, would prepare to drive us to school. Those were life-saving moments for me. Patricia my friend was a beautiful black woman, whose smile, revealing a tiny diastema, could lighten up a room. Our connection was uncomplicated at our first meeting in Culinary Arts Class. I believe she took a liking to me because I sort of assumed the position of a supportive older brother in her life. The boreholes in school were the 'manpower' models. the kind with a protruding vertical lever which required every ounce of energy to drag down and up to permit the flow of water. I'd walk her to the borehole to assist her in pumping and even carry the water to her block when necessary. Pat, I was learning, was an absolute '*Dadaba*' (a pampered rich kid) who craved some independence. She opted for Ho Polytechnic because she wanted to be far away from home, away from all the pampering, away from the 24-hour chauffeur and cleaning service. Her path wouldn't have been an option for me if I had been in her shoes. She was simply captivated by the idea of being around new people, making new friends and fending for herself outside the confines of her home. Well, sort of. She based most of her decisions on growing through life rather than going through it. Being away from her parents for the first time was a challenge she gladly embraced and executed to perfection. Pat had it easy with the boys on campus, especially Ben and Jonathan. To her, I was the older brother with whom she felt safe and could set apart from the rest of the boys in school. To quote her very words, I was "one cool guy who revealed a sense of seriousness and commitment in all practicals taught in class, and that was the driving force of our friendship. She recalls some days when she would walk together with Bernard and Jonathan to town whenever she desperately needed to purchase some groceries and other foodstuffs. A call to her parents would have had it sorted out but her first taste of "freedom" ignited a newness which made her gravitate towards blending in with the likes of us. I.B Philips, her father, originally founded Wise Way Cleaners. His company at the time provided laundry services to Lever Brothers Ghana ltd, a top-notch manufacturing company in Ghana which eventually transitioned into Unilever Ghana. In addition to Pat and her two siblings, Mr. Philips had ten other children he had fathered with other women. The wealth he had accumulated entirely from his business was reflected in the standard of living of all his kids. And like Patricia, they never had to break a nail to clean or walk for miles in the scorching sun to purchase an item. Some families may tussle for properties after a breadwinner's demise to keep up with a certain lifestyle, yet the physical absence of Pat's father at some point did not by any means create some sort of financial crisis. Her mother was the proprietor and founder of Faith Way School, located at Kwashieman, Accra. She also operated a cafeteria at the front of her Awudome home, where she baked and sold scones and other finger foods.

There was no rushing a conversation with Madam Azah at the cafeteria. Every question she'd ask was followed by sub-questions, a body text plus a conclusion before moving on to the next topic for discussion while we baked. On days I would go pay Pat a visit on vacations, she would engage my 'expertise' in preparing various baked goods at the cafeteria. I discovered just how great she was at holding conversations. Slowly, I found myself opening up and going along with every subject she'd put on the table for discussion. There was always some natural resistance to revealing my truth, somehow, over time, she had managed to wear that wall down to comprehend my being and also get to understand me better as a person than just being a friend to Patricia. Awudome had become home to me. Pat continued on her quest to stay completely away from home. Upon graduating from Ho Polytechnic, She took off to the Western Region of Ghana to again pursue catering at the Takoradi Polytechnic. Bagging that certificate, meant coming back to the confines of her home or seeking out a job closer to home, yet she was not done. She got enrolled at Kumasi Polytechnic in the Ashanti Region to study an HND in catering after which she signed up for her national service with the Young Women Christian Association (YWCA) in Adabraka, Accra. There was no stopping her! She settled back home after many years to assist her mother and brother in operating Faith Way School, A job she's proudly held for the past twelve years even after Madam Azah passed away in July 2021. Empathy was greatly a hallmark she effortlessly depicted in her actions towards me. There's no recollection of a time I was made to feel lesser than a person or judged for my lower standards of living. It still didn't make sense how God had strategically planted genuine helpers at every point in my journey to aid lighten my load.

Vacations from Ho Poly could last as long as 3 months. Rather than stay idle at home or shuffle between Awudome and 37 military housing, I'd sometimes go seeking an internship with various hospitality establishments. Almost every vacation, I worked with Shangri-La Hotels and Liberty Court Hotel both in Accra interchangeably. Though not on payroll, there was this glimmer of hope in looking forward to heading out to work every day. It might have been my soul's way of avoiding idleness which may eventually pave way for unnecessary thinking. I worked in the kitchen with the other cooks and chefs basically as their helping hand. It certainly was a great way of acquiring first-hand practical knowledge on creating some continental delicacies and enhancing my African cuisine skills.

On days I wanted to exhibit some tough skin on campus, I'd go mingle with the 'other' rich kids for a little spark. We brought the school to a standstill one day when we staged a demonstration against the administration and management for the poor quality of meals served at the dining hall among things we felt were being handled poorly. We were apprehended and arraigned before the disciplinary committee. Now, this was where reality came knocking. We were all placed on equal suspension but, my well-to-do friends after a phone call to their families, got their verdicts overturned within 24 hours. Who could I call? It was quite an unfortunate turn of events. The goal was to leave a mark in the school but not in this manner. The line was drawn. I knew where I belonged in an instant. As naive as I was, I thought the parents of my colleagues would include me in their plea yet I was wrong. The absence of an advocate in my case landed me back home on suspension. Before my suspension, I was made to crack stones at the school's new construction site. If I'm not exaggerating, their quantities were as much as half a truck which obviously would have taken me months to complete. At the time, Ho Tech was transitioning into Ho Polytechnic. Hence, a portion of the vast land had been dedicated to the construction of new blocks and facilities to usher in the change. Quickly, I gathered some money from sympathizers enough to hire some locals from the town to assist me to get the job done. Where were my accomplices? A flashback to my moment with Aunty Ruby came flooding my thoughts. It was fair to say I had been carried away by the false sense of belonging conferred on me by the so-called bond I shared with my colleagues. I paid a high price for an offence we committed together as a team.

Like it was for a lot of guys, the tertiary school was a place I intended to explore to the fullest. Every nook and cranny to me was a call for adventure. My thirst for "an experience" nearly got me caught up with the wrong side of the law. This was during my final year in school. I remember staying back on campus on one vacation with a few of those colleagues I embarked on a demonstration. We would sneak out into Ho town for a bit of a fun night. On one of such nights, we found ourselves in some sort of nightclub. I think it was called the Red Onion. Mobile phones were just becoming popular and owning one was a big deal as they were quite pricey for the average-earning Ghanaian. Loud music, dancing and the stench of local beverages could pretty much sum up the scene of a local Ghanaian nightclub. It was quite packed with a few older folks and more young folks like me who sought to have a good time. Someone's mobile phone got stolen. Everyone was thrown into a panic. Bags were searched and pockets were being dug to fish out the unfortunate thief. I freely allowed them to entirely search my bag and clothes because I had nothing to hide, at least that's what I thought till the lost phone rang. The owner of the phone had borrowed someone else's and dialled his number, to my utter dismay the lost phone rang loudly from my pocket like a baby on the verge of being kidnapped. You can't imagine the shock and horror on my face when I was hooked by the collar from behind like a criminal. Felt so surreal. I struggled to find balance in that chaotic situation. I was like one who dreamt. The police were summoned to the scene and placed me under immediate arrest. I informed Aunty Ruby of the mishap in school, which was immediate, followed by several phone calls to the few lawyers and judges she knew. It was safe to inform her first because I pictured exactly how my mother would have taken it. We lived on a budget back home so it would have been insane to dump an issue which required extra spending in fees. Within 24 hours I was discharged by the police and released by the school authorities to go home till the investigations were done. Arch Bishop Nicholas Duncan Williams of the Action Chapel used to hold prayer sessions on Thursdays dubbed "Prayer line." we would partake in the weekly prayer service with hopes that God would intervene on my behalf. Yes! I needed God now. Ironically, I was neither into prayer nor had any intention of pursuing a relationship with God. Yes, He existed and was the provider of our daily needs but nothing deeper beyond that. I had behaved selfishly in a moment without considering the stress I could put my family through. Giving in to the whims of my desires was about to cost me my DREAM and with shame repeatedly Knocking on my conscience, I had to seek the good God of Grace.

In between prayer sessions and sitting at home in bouts of sweats and anxiety, I reported at given intervals to the police station as they continued to investigate the matter. I knew I was innocent yet it would take some sort of miracle to prove how the phone ended up in my pocket. After Six months of investigations, the police explained how one of my friends stole the device from its owner only to plant it on me to save himself when the search began. UNBELIEVABLE, I could not fathom how a 'friend' could find it so easy to drag me down to pin a crime he had committed on me. I was awakened to the harsh realities of life, perhaps this was God's way of teaching me a lesson on trust and good company. I had been brought to the near end of myself to understand how to depend on Him. Aunty Ruby walked hand in hand with me through the uncertainties till we had a verdict. That woman undeniably played an instrumental role in keeping me on the right track toward achieving my goal. Perhaps, she saw something worth nurturing in me.

I studied in the most evident educational ways possible. Studying late into the night, joining study groups with leading "intellectuals" with enough capacity to assist in my weak subject areas in addition to overstaying my time at the Library adjacent to the shaded lovers' bench area. This was the finals of the catering course at Ho Polytechnic and I had a job to nail it. It was mid-1991, if my memory serves me right, the PNDC had announced its acceptance of the multi-party system in Ghana and the nation was heading towards its first Republic Day celebrations. Looking back at all the struggles faced, the humiliation suffered and endless hours dedicated to bettering my grades. The goal to succeed at the eleventh hour was clear. For whatever areas I had fallen short academically, I would ask for help from various coursemates where necessary to catch up. Still, it was almost unfeasible to cram in everything all at once. You could almost hear a pin drop on campus, it was all still. Haphazard movements on campus had ceased with all directions steered towards the nearest libraries and classrooms.

Three weeks later it was all over. We had completed the full chapter in Ho Poly after what seemed like an endless episode of brain torture. Like with every school, it was purely emotional, but we feigned the satisfaction of "finally leaving" the confines of campus. We had a few days to finalize our clearance proceedings, bid our farewells and exit the premises. I was clueless as to what lay ahead of me or what next to do with my life. It was obvious I had completed all final examinations with high hopes of excelling but didn't comprehend what next the drive was geared towards. The school emptied gradually as students rolled out the exit with a certain beam of pride. All personal acquired catering practical equipment which were still in good condition were packed at the bottom of my trunk followed by some books and finally my remaining good clothes. Flashbacks from my first journey to Ho, through to the fun and gut-wrenching times flooded my mind. It still felt like yesterday when I found myself in the mud for staging demonstrations with my peers. It was time to walk out of this school which had given me first-hand lessons on what life in the real world away from home was truly about. I walked out of the school wearing all the scars from those dark times with pride. A new walk to an uncertain tomorrow had begun as I took the first step out of the confines of Ho Polytechnic. I was truly going to miss this place.

# Chapter 5

# Chapter 5

It was still the second half of 1991 and we had about roughly a year to the release of our results. With more than enough time on my hands, I joined the thousands of graduates nationwide in search of an internship. Have you ever found yourself stuck at a point in time in your life where all you wanted to do was run, hide or even disappear from the surface of the earth? Well, that was me after school, coming back home to the same old impoverished situation drove me into a wall. Perhaps it's safe to say I was blinded by my burning desire for financial freedom. Upon successfully securing an internship with the African Academy of Music and Arts (AAMA) at Kokrobite, I quickly packed some clothes and dashed out to what I presumed would mark a new beginning. Mediocrity wasn't something I intended to accommodate on a long-term basis. *"Ah God, how bad have I offended you? Whatever did I do wrong to deserve a life of shame as this?'* my mother wailed. To her, she had lost everything. Ben had equally become rebellious and had shut everyone out while I had taken off to a place she knew nothing of. Grief placed her on the verge of taking her own life. Before you say anything, I'm not as insensitive as you're probably thinking. I had not premeditated an agenda to inflict pain on my mother. She had been through enough. She managed to put on a garment of strength each day as she hustled to fend for us, it was hard to watch. Her brawls with hardships made me ache in ways I never had. The quest for a better life in addition to the ugly tasks of constantly pondering over why and how my aunties and cousins had a better standard of living than we did, had driven me out of the house as an outcast. But I was hungry – hungry for success – in addition to the conviction of knowing I was going to be celebrated someday. The distance from Accra to Kokrobite, about 31 km via the George W. Bush highway was approximately an hour's drive. This physical distance from home would take a toll on my relationship with Ben and mar the enviable bond we once shared. The love we shared fizzled out with time as the insecurities and demands of adulthood reared their ugly heads upon both of us. Out of sight became out of mind as the years would roll by.

The African Academy of Arts which lay on the Accra-Cape Coast-Mankessim road embodied the spirit of Africa. It was founded by Mustapha Tettey Addy, one of Africa's well-known innovative composers in 1988. Before the establishment of AAMA, Kokrobite could be likened to one of the slumbering towns in Ghana. The Institution showcased crafted arts, cultural exhibitions and dance, music and food which at the time portrayed Ghana and Africa in a way as never seen before. Large number of tourists from various countries would troop in every week for a feel of what the academy had to offer – a touch of Africa, so the resorts were almost always fully booked. Immediately, I was assigned a role as a dishwasher. It wasn't what I'd preferred but it kept me away from over thinking. I had created a hallmark of being diligent in whatever I laid my hands on, especially when it's in connection with my purpose. Dishwashing had become the latest addition to my repertoire I equally executed to perfection. After work, I would lodge in a room at the AAMA resort with a grounded intention of never going back to 37 Military Barracks. This was my new home. My dedication and commitment to cleaning used dishes did not go unnoticed. After a year of sticking faithfully with this routine, I got promoted to a cook. Young Chef Francis had been born at last! Recollecting all I had learnt from Grandma Maku and Aunty Ruby at South Labadi, in addition to what I had garnered from Ho Poly, enabled my transition into a meister in the kitchen with display of finesse coupled with undeniable confidence by the stove in my chef's attire. This was all I hoped to be... a chef. For all that, I am yet to meet an underpaid dedicated chef like young Chef Francis Otoo in the 90s. The management of AAMA maintained me at the post for the next 12 months till I was given the ultimate promotion to Head Cook in 1993. It felt good to have been appreciated and recognized for my skills outside of my home.

A taste of the real world inside AAMA had erased the lingering thoughts of awaiting my results from Ho Poly temporarily. As announcements of the release of our results spread among tertiary students nationwide in 1992, I realized in a brief moment that, life, as it was in Kokrobite, was but for a little while. By the time I had gone back to Ho Polytechnic to check on my results, I already had an idea of what I wanted to read next. The plan was to hold on to my job at the AAMA, enrol in a school within Accra or its environs and strategically manage the time I would shuffle in between both schedules. The issue was back to the probabilities of taking my education further. I felt a dark cloud slowly flood my little sunshine. With years of surviving hardships to my credit, I had slowly in one way or the other, gotten around to holding myself back from slipping down the road of despair or surrendering to my lowest instincts. Upon realizing I had passed my finals beyond expectations, I held discussions with Uncle Seth on securing aid to further my education. Uncle Seth in his affluent days managed to pull some strings to get me into Accra Polytechnic to read Catering Stroke II. Financial Aid from my uncle went as far as paying for my fees. It required me to work harder to make ends meet to fund all commutes to school.

Accra Polytechnic sat on Barnes Road in Accra, about 25.4 km from Kokrobite. Blending in with other freshmen in school wasn't such a hard thing to do. Working constantly in a new environment with new people on a daily at AAMA had slowly brought out an extroverted side of me. I had gotten quite familiar with most of my mates by the end of the first week of orientation. We were pretty hanged on one another, though assigned to different classes. I would stay all weekend at the AAMA working 9 to 10 hours on Fridays, Saturdays and Sundays. On weekdays, I'd get on the 56mins ride on a *tro-tro* from Kokrobite to Accra to perch in hostels around campus with some friends. There were times I'd walk from the school's premises to Kaneshie station which was about 21 minutes away from the school, to board a Kokrobite-bound vehicle— a routine I kept up till my final year in school. It turned out that there was still a lot I had to study about life away from home in the 90s, mastering the art of being okay with having less than others and just being "okay" with struggling to survive. The other guys in school seemed content with their lives. Whenever they had needs, all they needed to do was to ask their parents. That thought seemed almost laughable to me. Was I to call my mum or the man whose name I bore, yet wanted nothing to do with us? Did I make mention of the time away from Osu Home School where Ben and I unleashed hell on our mother for "concealing" the identity of our father? Well, allow me to fill you in. That was around my second year at Ho Polytechnic, before my brother and I became estranged. I had come home for a vacation after yet another hectic Semester. Questions surrounding the absence of our father still lingered, both at school and at home. I spent most months of a year away from home in a place where parents visited their wards almost every weekend with food, gifts etc. I had people questioning the whereabouts of my parents, precisely, of my father. There were times my friends would throw jabs at me concerning his absence, to shatter my sense of worth. It was the same story back home. Seemed to us like there had been a general announcement on how we had been discarded by our father. Dreadful was the perfect fit for our feeling of otherness. Ben and I had had enough, we demanded answers. I seized a machete while Ben grabbed a kitchen knife and dashed to the room where our mum was resting her tired feet. "What's going on?" she asked shakily. Pointing the machete to her neck, I demanded the whereabouts of our father. We were not two grown men who had a relationship with their living father nor had a clear memory of him. We knew there was a back story to this silent vendetta he held against us. In tears, my mother explained the issue of how she had dropped out of the military academy as a sacrifice to support my father graduate from the same academy. Right from our infancy, our father had been non-existent. Previous to our conception, my parents in their early to mid-20s had begun planning their wedding. My mother describes feeling completely over the moon with all the intimate hours they both spent visualizing their matrimony. Then the threats started rolling in. One fine afternoon, a lady barged into her home to issue a word of caution against proceeding with her marriage preparations to her fiancé, my father, because there was a forthcoming nuptial between my dad and another woman, a biracial one to be precise…shocking! My mother highly doubted that the man in whose arms she rested could betray her this way. Had she been playing second fiddle the entire time? True to the reports, he walked the other woman down the aisle. When that marriage hit the rocks after a few years, he came back to my mother on his knees, a while later, Ben was conceived. Despite his disability, Ben was wholeheartedly accepted by my father, he was his son after all. Two years later my mother discovered that she had taken seed again. This was a couple of months after my father had been sent on a mission. She wasn't

aware, she couldn't tell because she had no symptoms. She kept my father in the dark while moving along to schedule an abortion. "An abortion! Why?" I asked in a disheartened tone. She failed to explain. She had developed complications after an initial failed attempt to snuff the life out of the baby on her own. While on admission, a nurse at the hospital tipped my father off on my mother's situation.
"Pregnant! She's pregnant?"
"Yes sir, I just had to inform you." She replied
"Impossible! I have been away for months so how's that baby mine? Kindly inform her to find the father of that child she's carrying."
He continued, "I do not own that pregnancy, besides, she had only been over to see me once since my departure."
The line went dead right after. Baffling right? I thought it only took a single encounter to bear a child. He had vehemently denied being my father from birth. After a safe delivery, Lt Col Nicholas Otoo had still shown no interest in seeing his newborn. However, his father visited to see for himself, the child Nicholas had wanted nothing to do with. "*Ah* Nick is misbehaving!" he exclaimed upon setting eyes on the child. "This is my grandson," he added after noticing the striking resemblance between his son and the child he denied. "I need to talk some sense into Nicholas immediately." My mother could only nod in agreement with the hope that he will indeed honour his promise and get Nick to come to see his son. After 3 months, there stood my paternal grandfather with his brother at the door, geared up to perform my naming ceremony without my father. To deepen the wounds, Nicholas had stopped supporting my mother with whatever kind of help he used to send prior to my birth. The disgrace. The deception. They cut so deep that my mother could neither inform her siblings nor her parents. She paused in her narrations to stare deep into my eyes. The pain was evident and sincere. "Look,"

she said, "even your demeanour, height, stature and mannerisms are your dad's entirely. You took them all." She tried making sense of my father's actions and sought to make excuses for why he did what he did to his family.

As the story got deeper, she called on Aunty Ruby to come by to aid her and explain how the absence of our father was no fault of hers. To cap it all, his desire to completely cut us off began before we could recite the alphabet. It wasn't what we had hoped to hear but it was somewhat a relief to understand that it was no fault of ours…it was all him.

Infuriated, I made my way to the Accra High Court in search of a lawyer with no legal fees in possession. I was directed to the office of a young lawyer who hastily inquired about my reason for being there, to him, I was "quite young" to solicit the services of a legal practitioner.
"Okay Young man, what can I do for you?" he asked with an arch in his left brow.
"I'm here to bring my father to Justice."
I replied with every sense of seriousness in me. I elaborated on my reasons and told him everything my mum and Aunt had shared. He deserved to face the law for neglecting his responsibilities as a father in addition to all the hardships and mockery he had subjected us to.
"Are you okay?" he asked. "C'mon get out of my office. You little boy have no idea what you're demanding. Stop spewing nonsense and exit."
And so that day, I made a deal with myself not to get drowned in my emotions towards my father. Focusing on the hurt caused me to always react in ways which only pulled embarrassment me.

Just when I was about to let go of the unfortunate incident, Uncle

Seth offered to take a day off his many schedules to drive me to Cape Coast where our dad resided at the time with his other family. Ben at the time had killed all interest in seeing him so as Uncle Seth drove towards our home, he bolted. On the other hand, I badly desired to know the man I looked like. How satisfying it would be to get acquainted with the other half of my lineage. My heart pounded, and my thoughts raced throughout the journey. Anxiety had the best of me. I dreaded the encounter yet I thought it best to get some answers from the man in question and lay this issue to rest once and for all. My stomach turned. What if he wasn't excited about the idea of getting acquainted with his now mature son? Scenes from our encounter at the American Embassy flooded my mind; perhaps his reaction would be different this time. I was utterly dismayed when he drove us out of his residence and stated emphatically that he wanted nothing to do with us. It was all the confirmation we needed to finally conclude that again, it was no fault of ours after all. He was the culprit. Suddenly, I felt bad for our mother for succumbing to a false narrative that this man presented as love to her in the past. Though enraged, it was all the closure we needed.

...

Staying in touch with some colleagues from Ho Polytechnic was a hectic task to keep up with, no wonder I'm terrible at recalling the names of most people I had met on my journey. However, breaking communication with Pat Biney and her mum was almost impossible. There was a certain degree of gratitude I showed towards those who held up the lights to my path, considering how supportive they had been, I maintained contact with them. Patricia Biney still studied in the same catering field as me. As in the Ho Polytechnic, whenever it was time to go shopping for her school practical items, her mother would provide double with the money required to shop for my set as well. Her generous gesture of sponsoring all my practical expenses was repeated almost throughout my three-year stay at Accra Polytechnic. It was not burdensome for Madam Azah to splurge on my academics and upkeep. After all, I was considered and treated in the likeness of her only biological, Botwe. Their level of generosity and empathy was matchless. They were simply God-sent.

Like other good students in my class of 1994, I got the chance to partake in external practical jobs to earn a little income. Mrs Laine, the principal of the Catering school at Accra Polytechnic always treated the best performing students in her class to meagre working opportunities outside the campus. You'd see us dressed like the professionals we aspired to be, away from the regular pair of denim trousers and t-shirts we'd often wear to class, to serve our guests with whatever Mrs Laine made available to us. I loved the feeling of being out in the open, away from the AAMA kitchen or the confining spaces of our classrooms— the feelings those experiences brought are difficult to blot out. It was belonging to your own little community governed by merit. Mrs Laine gathered her team after school one Friday to give us a brief on a contract she had secured for the weekend at the Ford Foundation on the University of Ghana campus, about a few meters away from the Legon Hall Annex. It was the wedding of Mrs Ambassador Martha Ama Pobee. The diplomat who would later become Ghana's first female Permanent Representative to the United Nations for five years from 2015. From 2006 - 2010, she served as the head of chancery at the Embassy of Ghana in Washington. After successfully ending her toll of duty, she returned to foreign ministries in Accra as the director of public affairs. She served as the acting High commissioner in Pretoria, South Africa for two years, after which she was appointed ambassador to New York. At the writing of this book, she serves as United Nations Assistant Secretary-General for Africa where she focuses on peace-building and operations, and conflict prevention to address the root causes and triggers of conflict in Africa. She was set to be wed to the late Mr. John Samuel Pobee who was an Anglican priest and Emeritus Professor. As the official wait team of the ceremony, we were to arrive at the premises before set up was completed to usher in guests. As they trooped into the cocktail décor style area, I'd occasionally scan the rest of the room, perhaps to see if I'd spot a familiar face. The audacity, as if I run in the same circles of affluence. It wasn't the usual sit-down wedding ceremony with an introduction of the chairman, and all other expected 'order of ceremony' for a typical Ghanaian wedding, which always ends with guests struggling for their share of the buffet of local Ghanaian dishes. No, we had Hors d'oeuvres passed around. Canapés, mozzarella sticks with dips, Virginia ham and white cheddar croquettes, roasted garlic and sweet potato crostini among other fancy finger foods. The reception was simple yet spectacular. Classic Ghanaian music played softly in the background. We served wine, champagne, and some soft drinks to the guests who walked from one table to the other exchanging pleasantries and others keenly building on social connections. Again— it was nothing like your typical Ghanaian wedding plus it was the morning of a weekday. Definitely not the kind intended to attract all the attention.

Recollecting memories from her wedding, Ambassador Pobee tells me much later that she only noticed me as the boy with his head sticking above everyone else's. Just going through her wedding photo album at her home in DC, she exclaimed, "*ah* I know this guy… of course that's Francis."

For me, the wedding was just another occasion to get paid, another hustle in my desperation to survive, but as they say, the steps of a man are ordered by the Lord. Unbeknownst to me, Ambassador Martha Pobee, the bride of the day, would show up later up the ladder of my career in a different light, in a new space to literally keep me on the path of my purpose.

*There she is! The Matriarch of the Abadji family, the one with whose umbrella I developed the love for cooking... my late grandmother, Janet Maku Abadji.*

*My grandma Maku and her husband, my late grandfather, Mr. Gilbert Baah Abadji, loved to wear cloths "to match" for Sunday church service.*

*A 2 month old me with my three year old brother, Kwesi Andoh-Otoo of blessed memory in 1997*

*A smiling Victoria Larko Abadji, my mother, photographed with her two boys, showcasing them with pride.*

*If there was one thing my mother knew best to do, it was to rock her army uniform with very well and with pride.*

*Here she is again! Sitting at her desk in her office at the 37 Military barracks. As a matter of fact, this woman was the first image of what a hardworking woman truly is and what they represent.*

*Mama Victoria Abadji, the retired army officer and the 80 year old who today, has become my friend, my adviser and partner in prayer. This photograph was taken in July 2022, minutes after she sat for the hour long conversation surrounding my birth.*

*Ho Technical University (HTU), where it all began. The gateway to honing the culinary skill implanted in me by my late grandmother.*

*A student's guide to navigating the nooks and crannies of my alma mater; the HTU campus map, an alumni initiative, I hear, is making trekking through campus easier.*

*The old boys' dormitory I was registered throughout my stay at HTU. It has been refurbished a number of times and continues to accommodate students till date.*

*This area photographed holds a lot of memory. The lovers' bench area of HTU, adjacent the old library was a spot for young lovers seeking to rekindle their spark, for parents waiting to see their wards and for regular students who just wanted to while away time on a Saturday afternoon.*

*This reservoir stood prior to my admission to HTU and continues to stand in 2022. This symbolized survival for every student at Ho Technical University because it served as an emergency supply to all campus residences whenever the mechanical water pump failed.*

*The Esther Nkulenu Demonstration restaurant, held all cooking practicals and culinary activities for all catering students at HTU.*

*Unlike in my time at HTU, culinary students get to choose and study from a wide range of courses around the subject of food, at the Department of Food Science and Technology on the HTU campus.*

*Wow! This photograph... the memories keep coming in. This kitchen was one of the few available to us at HTU, to carry food practicals.*

*Ah! Patricia Biney ($2^{nd}$ right), the friend who made me family and welcomed me to her home. I can't really recall my reason for looking away from the camera. This was at her mother's Awudome residence, during her Presbyterian confirmation party.*

*Yes! I remember this one. It was the part, again at Pat's confirmation party, where I overtook the little girl on my right to serve myself at the buffet.*

*She held me down in my low moments in Ho Poly, she continues on social media to show love to my craft. Patricia Biney, still, is one of my closest friends. Wherever my story is shared, it would be highly impossible to complete the narration without her name being mentioned.*

*Accra Polytechnic, currently Accra Technical University; Here, I was presented with rare opportunities to serve gatherings of diplomats and hone my skills for the real culinary world.*

*The ever gorgeous Aunty Ruby Abadji, the last of my mother's siblings and my culinary buddy from my days at South Labadi Estates. Count on this woman to throw in words of wisdom on your blue days. She knows just what to say and when to say it!*

*No, this is not an old photo of me; it is that of my uncle, Seth Abadji, The senior of the Abadji siblings, my friend and an early believer of my dreams.*

# Part 2

# Against All Odds

# Chapter 6

# Chapter 6

As the months continued to roll by I realized the mundane, humdrum existence I was living. Going in for Madam Laine's waiting gigs, commuting to school from Kokrobite and working part-time as a cook at the African Academy of Arts (AAMAs) pretty much marked my weekly activities till our final exam. Leisure was a luxury I simply could not afford. I had chosen to leave home with an empty pocket in the pursuit of success. I put this on myself, a pressure to not drive my life and career into a wreck.

There was never ample time to study but I did have my ways. So when it came to the final exam, I was not at all terrified. I emerged with distinction from the 1994 final exams in catering II at Accra Polytechnic and began settling into my permanent working life. Graduation came with its demands, it was a requirement to pay for the garment, pay for clearance among other things I can barely recall. My issue as you have come to understand was always about money. It seemed like the subject just hated being around me. They *do everything on your* attitude I had inculcated made it difficult to call on any of my relatives for whatever little support they could put together for me. Again, it was the desire to not be an extra burden which sort of kept me away from constantly asking for support. With that, I failed to participate in the graduation ceremony and had to wait for years before I was able and ready to clear those debts for the release of my certificate. My mother, however, continued to stay in touch with me. Ben was still alive during this period, this was between

1994/1995 and we were both still yet to bridge the invisible gap which had kept us apart from each other. The initial interest we had both shared in each other's lives, had died with time. Occasionally, whenever I'd visit home, we'd say a thing or two to each other and go about our dealings.
The African Academy of Arts (AAMAs) had become a comfort zone, and as they say about comfort zones, they stifle growth. The search for a new working opportunity continued throughout the additional
one-and-a-half year period I stayed at the AAMAs post-graduation, till an offer from Golden Tulip Hotel in Accra presented itself.

The 4-star Hotel which sits by the Liberation Road in Accra was and is still one of the finest Hospitality establishments in Ghana. Though only10 minutes away from the city centre, the hotel boasts of a serene ambience beautifully landscaped over capacious compounds. I gained the life-changing opportunity to work with the kitchen staff as a cook in 1996. Moving in with the desire and hunger to attain greatness, I went in as a vibrant young man ready to showcase my skills and worth to Whom It May Concern me that I was cut out for more than I appeared. I deliberately made the effort to invest my all into becoming the highest version of myself, the self-actualised man who had it all. Through my efforts, I was named the worker of the month and eventually, cook of the year after 12 months with the establishment. I had still not moved back in with my family, though resigning from the AAMA had revoked my access to the staff chamber at the resort which had served as my home over the past few years. This time, I hopped from friend to friend as a squatter in their rented apartment. Mentally, I had cast myself out of home because I had grown accustomed to the war I had waged against poverty which in turn birthed a goal of only going back home a success. It felt like I had grown to believe other people's version of my truth, that I was never good enough, so naturally, there was a burning desire to be something...anything.

My drive as a cook made an impression on Mr. Ofori, the head chef at Golden Tulip Accra. He got me immediately promoted to the cold room, where salads and sandwiches were made. I would say I got bumped into the 'fancy' space out of his pure admiration for my work ethic. Mr. Ofori eventually became my mentor who personally took me beneath his wings to give me up close directives on my career as a chef. Those were priceless moments I still hold so dear. He was an accomplished man who, I suppose, sought to pass down what he had learnt over the years to someone with the same zeal and enthusiasm he had commenced his career with. It was always the smallest things which made the most mark. I mostly went home with a sense of importance — again, someone had noticed the spark I had managed to keep alive over the years. Complacency never got the best of me, I still stayed on my grind and kept the hustle up yet, it looked to others as though, I was in a series of fortunate twists when I got promoted to the position of assistant banquet chef. In the kitchen, I primarily assisted the head banquet chef in overseeing the quality and consistency of foods prepared for all banquets and events. In addition to all that, I assisted in the direction and organisation of other employees at the banquet kitchen. My experience at the Hotel was quite a golden one. We catered and served several high-profile events which gave me some exposure to the Ghanaian cuisine community, including one of the birthday celebrations of H.E Nana Addo Dankwa Akuffo Addo at his residence before he assumed Presidential Office. In all of my grapples with life, Love was an area I was yet to explore to the fullest. My years had been drowned in sweats of "workaholism" which afforded me little to no room to survey the possibilities in that area.

**Sarah Vroom** was an enthusiastic young lady in the banquet kitchen. She possessed an uncommon seriousness for a young lady in her 20s. With the way she carried herself on duty and executed her daily tasks with grace and poise, she drew my attention with ease. 'Who's that girl?' I asked a colleague one day, 'oh that's Miss Vroom. She's with the banquet kitchen,' he replied. I could finally put a name to the face which often made me skip a pulse. Sarah was a beautiful averaged height dark skinned lady with a smile which always lit up a room. There was an internal pressure to get acquainted. Like a Private Investigator, I observed she had a good rapport with Juliana Frimpong and Eunice Ocloo, both my chef superiors in the kitchen. In a bid to satisfy my curiosity, I walked to Julie one working break to express my interest in being friends with Sarah. As a man, you'd expect me to make an instant approach, throw in some moves and sweep her off her pretty feet with the expected smooth lines yet. I didn't have the guts to. I'm sure it was an issue of self-esteem, given my persistent struggles with accommodation, validation and finances but when the heart 'wants what it wants,' even the most bothersome predicaments go into the blur. There was just something about the way she would walk across the kitchen stylishly pushing her trolley packed with the plates of salads I had gladly arranged for her, towards the banquet hall. I would offer to get the elevator for her sometimes and would occasionally flash a nervous grin she barely even noticed. Upstairs a few times at the banquet hall, after I had voluntarily offered to ride with her in the elevator, she'd give stern instructions on where and how to place the salads and other meals on the table. We worked in separate spaces; I at the kitchen and she at the banquet hall. Major events at Golden Tulip created brief moments to share with Sarah. Today, she maintains her stance that she barely took notice of me. To her, I was just another chef in uniform, just another 9 to 5 worker at the hotel. Sarah, I had learnt was an introvert. There were some personal struggles with socializing and allowing people into her space, which she delightfully terms as "*observing before taking the leap*." She remembers the moment her best friend at the time, Eunice, approached her with an appeal on my behalf.

"Sarah," she called before leaning against the wall of the empty banquet hall. "Can't you tell Chef Francis likes you?"

"Chef Francis?" she asked with her eyes alert in a curious expression. She demanded further clarification.

"Yes! The tall dark, handsome chef at the kitchen downstairs, *mepakyew* don't tell me you haven't noticed him."

"Well I have seen him at post a few times but that's all there is to it," Sarah replied.

Eunice continued with persuasion, "He pleaded with me to inform you of his feelings towards you. Sister, I think he likes you."

"Okay. I don't see any wrong in that. Everybody likes everybody. It's no big deal."

"*Eii* Sarah, stop saying that. You mean you are yet to notice how he looks at you from across the room whenever you walk through those kitchen doors?" Eunice asked standing akimbo at this point.

"Eunice, please relax. The truth is I haven't taken the time to give him a second look. I only go down there to gather my salads to present at the banquet that's all… *ooh*! So that's why he's been overly helpful to me? I had no idea."

Sarah wasn't wrong. I hadn't been up to anything special to separate me from the other men in the kitchen. The only words she had ever said to me thus far were, "where are my salads?" They slid like a song from her lips.

With no time to back down, new schemes to win her affection or at least get her to return my smiles dawned on me. I had conceived what I thought was a great idea— it was to sneak into the kitchen after banquet parties to whip something up for the entire banquet staff of which Sarah was a part. To me, it was the only way to get closer to her. On one of those expeditions, I suffered a minor accident. I injured my left thumb with a butcher's knife while trying to cut some chicken to prepare the secret meal of the day... and guess what? It caught Sarah's attention. I thought the meal would do it for me but I guess the injury broke the ice for me. This lady felt so awful about the injury that she offered to accompany me to the hospital to get stitched. That was a page out of a movie script where the protagonist gets to share an awkward moment with the woman of his dreams. I did not see a lady in her early 20s that night. I came face to face with a real woman, a rare quality in most women her age. She saw me through the reception, the OPD, the theatre and the exit. At the bus station, I gathered the courage to express my interest in getting to know her a little bit more than just work buddies. The injury had come at the right time in my quest to capture the heart of Sarah Vroom.

"Sarah... I must say that I'm grateful for taking me through the many medical formalities to get my stitches." I said with a hint of shyness.

"Don't mention at all Francis, I'm happy to help." She responded in a soft tone.

"Well... umm, Sarah I like you and I would love to be your boyfriend."

"My boyfriend? Francis, I honestly can't offer you anything beyond whatever friendship we are beginning to develop from this point." She responded firmly without a brush of doubt.

Whatever influenced me into thinking it was the right time to propose, I'll never know! There was a short silence before anyone could utter a word. It was clear she didn't want a romantic relationship with me which was quite disappointing. Life went by, work progressed yet my feelings for Sarah persisted. Our relationship stayed the same. Things certainly did not get awkward between us. however, I was still hesitant to take an 'L' and back down, I went further to dedicate my subsequent salary to purchasing endless yards of African print fabric to coax the lady of my dreams into reciprocating my love. Juliana stood a few meters away from the exit with eagerness. I had called on her assistance to deliver what I thought was a great gift to awaken the love of a woman. I implored her to get Sarah to change her mind about her earlier response to my proposal and she gave me her word. It was the longest 24 hours I've ever had to wait for anything yet Sarah insisted she wanted no part of it. Julie returned with the cloth still in its bag in hand to break the very obvious news that I had been turned down again. Pursuing Sarah was the next good thing I had going on besides my job and I wasn't prepared to back down. Harnessing all the boldness in me, I approached and asked her out on a date. Just as I expected, she was opposed to the idea but I assume my determination and masculine charms won her over for a date night. It was difficult to tell if she were as excited about the evening as I was, her facial expressions were quite unreadable. We both still had the night to decide on whether we would officially become an item or stay friends... technically, it was all up to her. I was the only constant in a love story yet to unfold.

"Where are you taking me Francis?" she asked with a smile, holding firmly to her hand. We complimented each other very well. In appearance, in our height variations and in the way our laughter always burst out in unison. "Let's go grab a drink there." I replied gesturing to the popular 'Alex Khebab' spot on the 37 roads, a few meters away from the hotel. The name clarifies exactly what was served at the spot. spicy hot goat, beef and chicken kebabs alongside bottles of chilled beer among a variety of soft drinks. It was the 'go-to' place for young couples or people looking to vibe their nights away in the company of beautiful people. Sarah looked beautiful, her dark skin glistened with the night as I observed her every little move while briefly disappearing into a reverie of what our future would look like together. Miss Vroom did have me by the heart, I was in love. Snapping out of it, I beckoned to a waiter to take our orders, a soft drink for my lady and a light beer for the gentleman. There's a swiftness to how time flies by when you're with the people you love. Those hours came by microseconds. That night, it became apparent that Sara had feigned her emotions towards whatever had grown between us. She felt it yet ignored it. I wondered how she managed to pull that through while I, on the other hand, was terrible at hiding my true sentiments. The highlight of the night was the unveiling of her true emotions. We sat beneath the moonlight with some cool highlife music playing over our lengthy conversations which were mainly centred on getting well acquainted with each other and unravelling what both of us were made of.

# Chapter 7

# Chapter 7

"Fine," She said with a straight stare. "If you're that interested in knowing where I live and genuine about your intentions concerning me, I would have to take you home to see my parents." I sat back in excitement as the realization of finally winning Sarah over hit me. Her response was a clear indication of her feelings and I was done awaiting clarity. Though a 23-year-old boy with nothing to his name, I knew what it meant to do right by a woman and I am currently of the belief that, God had placed me in a home with a single mother to observe everything it wasn't to love a woman so I could learn all it entailed to truly love one. I consented to go to see her parents as a friend. Being with Sarah kept my restlessness in check. The constant feeling of being anxious about success in my future seemed to fall away in her presence. There was a calm to her I couldn't fathom. She had a way of alluding to me without saying my name whenever anyone at the bar caught her attention or made a mockery of themselves in any manner, the long talks and laughter still echo through my mind now and then. The night winds got chilly and swift with whistling sounds as they blew against the trees. It had gotten quite late and Sarah needed to get home.

Sarah continues to echo today, that her feelings had flowered quickly after she realized how selfless I was. She claims to have taken note of how I humbly addressed my bosses and subordinates in the kitchen in addition to how I amicably resolved pressing issues among our colleagues and their respective superiors effortlessly. While some bosses were smitten by my charm, others were not particularly enthused by my presence. Ben Owusu was one of the few bosses I had in my corner. He was the banquet Manager and Sarah's immediate boss. News about Sarah and I being an "item" had spread among the staff at the hotel so it certainly struck a nerve when Ben Owusu began making advances at my lady and pushed it further by inviting her out on a platonic date. "What's harmless about inviting my woman to sit out for a drink at night?" I asked Sarah angrily after informing me of Ben's offer. "No no, do you need me to talk some sense into him?" His Audacity was deeply agitating. "Trust me...it's quite needless Joojo, please let me handle him," she replied. After being bluntly turned down, Ben Owusu hatched ways to render me silly and mostly incompetent in the eyes of my superiors. Regardless of his gimmicks, I still held a commanding lead in Sarah's eyes.

She said little on our way to her parent's house at Dansoman. This was about a week after our little date night at Alex Kebab. She perhaps feared how her family might receive me, though I looked all 'chill' and composed on the outside, I was crumbling on the inside. There's a natural uneasiness attached to meeting the family of one's love interest. The devouring concerns of how bad an introduction could go or the incessant thoughts of feeling out of place when given the subtle cold shoulder by a parent or the family altogether could mess up one's demeanour.
"*Ah* Abakumah Payin *woaba,* you're here." Madam Hammond said exchanging smiles with her daughter. *Payin?* I wondered. Sarah was a twin? I did not know that. In the Ghanaian Akan society, *Payin* is the title given to the elder of a twin, be it male or female... and Abakumah was her maiden name, Turned out my lady had showcased a mysterious character by keeping that on a

hush-hush. It impressed me. I noticed where Sarah derived her grace and charm. Mrs Hammond was quite welcoming, she exuded some confidence in her calm demeanour which I found remarkable. She smiled at me and gestured to a seat in the living room. A brief heavy silence covered the atmosphere.

"Do you care for some water or anything?" her mother asked with her chin slightly raised and pointing in my direction.
"I'm okay Ma. Thank you."
"Ma," Sarah chimed in with her face downcast, this is my friend and colleague, Francis. We both work at Golden Tulip."
"Oh okay… you're welcome Francis. Make yourself at home."
Sarah hadn't agreed to become my girlfriend yet but I guess madam Hammond got the memo— She had already figured out what was happening at that moment. Her father came in a while later followed by her twin sister, Ruby Vroom. I had never been to a trial in a courtroom but I assumed the feeling could be likened to how I felt at Sarah's home that day. Ruby, like her father Mr. Vroom, wasn't my biggest fan. I later came to know that Sarah was being cajoled by her family to marry a certain rich man at the time, No wonder Ruby would squeeze her brows and purse her lips with her eyes squint whenever I'd walk through the doors to visit Sarah. Francis became synonymous with the boulder Ruby needed to get out of the way for her sister to see the light.

With time, Sarah agreed to officially embrace the title of "a girlfriend." Took me long enough but she did me the honours of finally accepting my proposal. A new beginning demanded real honesty and transparency. Since it was the beginning of our courtship, Sarah let me in on her life story in a way she had never done. She had brought forth a child through no fault of hers…a daughter. She had been raped by a man she had wanted nothing to do with. At the time of the revelation, the child was over 6 months old.

"*Abakumah,*" I said reaching out for her hands. "Believe it when I say that I love you. I appreciate your honesty but it doesn't matter to me. My intentions have been evident from the onset. I love you and that is all that matters."

"Joojo but you..."

"But what Abakumah? If it implied doing the needful as a real man, I would."

"Hmm, I couldn't agree more Francis, if you want to be with me as you claim. I suggest that you go see my parents, this time as a man seeking my hand. It would be an honour on my family and your appreciation for our Christian family values."

Marriage was never a subject we danced about, we both knew exactly what we wanted and worked together to make it a reality. We both were quite young, yet I knew it was the right thing to do. My love for Sarah was quite intense and had no sense to it... it was strange yet in a really good way. When it came to our relationship, Sarah could already see right through me. She knew when I was telling a fib and when I was all above board. She was awed by my words because she could feel my sincerity. I proposed to her sometime in 1997 and became unofficially engaged. I had graduated to become somewhat the fiancé of my dream girl. Her daughter, Cecilia, became mine. I adopted and named her after me. Cecilia Otoo, my only daughter and the bright 20-year-old lady at Delaware University, USA, whom I have grown fond of and overly protective of. The sad part in all of these was the fact that I couldn't call my brother to gush over my feelings for my lady— how I had amusingly fallen in love with a woman who had my attention at first sight. We kept in touch somehow, but the bond we shared growing had slightly faded with time. The Ben I knew would have joked about how I had gotten turned down or how I had ridiculously dedicated my salary to acquiring a piece of cloth to win over the love of a woman, he would have had a field day.

Meanwhile, at Golden Tulip, we had received a new Executive Chef from Holland, his name was Paul Moulda. He saw to the many A-list functions for our clientele list. The Rotary club led by their Chairman at the time, the late Honorable Peter Ala Adjetey, the former speaker of parliament, held a successful banquet at the hotel. To appreciate the tremendous effort of the banquet staff, we were treated to good food and drinks on the house. After hours came the happy hour, per this reason, I quickly grabbed a cold can of beer to quench the flames of stress within. Along came Paul Mudda, who fumed at my "audacity" to consume alcohol at work. I did however enlighten him on the fact that it was after hours and per the rules governing the establishment, we were free to do as we liked. Yet Moulda wasn't about to let me go with ease, at least not without showing me "who's boss." He threw in many attempts to have me dismissed from Golden Tulip. I guess the heat generated from our little exchange of words before other staff members compelled him to show his mightiness. His outbursts were completely condescending which nearly extinguished my vibrant spirit. In a flash of rage, I pulled a knife on him while grabbing him by the collar. Had it not been for the intervention of everyone present, it would have probably turned bloody. He had singlehandedly unleashed the rebellion I had tried to overcome over the years. I fell under the impression that people had it in for me because of my rising potential in my field of work. With my target remaining to attain greatness and garner accomplishments, anyone who posed a threat to my goal had to be dealt with. Also, I believed that he had the 'hots' for my girlfriend. He probably couldn't stand the idea of her settling for a guy like me instead of him. Well, I might have been financially deprived but I did believe I was quite a catch. He had more reasons to write off my career. Seeing that I was a young chef highly revered by his employers for his impeccable skills and enthusiasm for work. If I were on the other side of the table, I would pose a threat to myself too. Most people did not see the reason for Sarah to settle *"with that boy,"* a title I was mostly referred to in their conversations, yet she wouldn't budge. The hurdles and trials had positively transformed our relationship into something beyond definition.

I recall those many nights when I'd sneak in with her into the house she lived with her parents after we got off work. We'd stay up all night talking about nothing. There's a thrill attached to young love. I bet it comes with some extra adrenaline which makes you feel invincible. My readiness to embark on something that could easily place our relationship in jeopardy was baffling. Madam Hammond caught us a few of those moments yet covered up for us. She believed her daughter had a future with me unlike the other members of her family. We fell into a ridiculous routine over the next few weeks: Going to work, talking on lunch breaks and several times over the phone, sneaking into her home to stay the night till 4 am the next day. It rolled over and over till we talked.

With time, Sarah and I realized that it was quite unhealthy for both our career and relationship to thrive in the same work establishment. There was a lot of truth to that because suddenly, the echo of Mudda's voice developed an all-new irritating timbre which quite became a trigger for my nerves— I needed to get out of there. He was still on the quest to get me kicked out of the tulip Accra.

Fortunately, in 1999, a new "It" place in the capital emerged with a big buzz. Information about cooks, chefs and other kitchen staffers being recruited spread like wildfire in the employee gossip pipeline. Already, I was in a bit of a puzzle as to where my next move would be. It had to be someplace similar to the Tulip or even better. I applied and got recruited almost immediately, Sarah on the other hand, stayed behind at the Golden Tulip while I tendered in my resignation to begin a new chapter with La Palm Royal beach Hotel. On my final day at the Tulip Accra, I brought Sarah along with me to a happy hour at Alex Khebab again to discuss the newness in our arrangements and the "what next" of our future together as a couple.

LA PALM ROYAL BEACH HOTEL sat adjacent to the popular Labadi beach on the No. 1 Bypass road in Osu and across from The La Trade Fair edifice. La Palm sat on a vast land of about 30 acres, overlooking the shores of the Atlantic Ocean with giant coconut trees surrounding the massive Greek-style swimming pool, which created lovely scenery. The hotel had about 150 rooms grouped under Presidential, Royal and junior suites with affordable standard rooms to suit the everyday Ghanaian.

October 1999 saw a gathering of newly recruited cooks and chefs from different establishments who had all converged under one roof with a common goal of seeking a new beginning in a fresh space. La Palm was quickly becoming a Principal place of gathering for businessmen and the crème de la crème of the society. A series of orientations were prearranged to prepare us for an incoming Head of States conference. Vigorous practical and theoretical training was carried out over a couple of days before being officially hired as a Supervisor for a section of the kitchen and handed a lead role as a cook for the Ecowas Summit, which saw a convergence of various heads of state and dignified figures from across Africa. The day finally came with a rush of protocol training, of course, it was nerve-wracking, it was the

# Chapter 8

# Chapter 8

I fondly recall the 22nd edition of the African Cup of Nations (AFCON) in January 2000, where both Ghana and Nigeria were pegged as the co-hosts of the prestigious all Nations tournament. It was the first time the confederation had ever awarded hosting privileges to two countries. It was a big deal for Ghana as the honour conferred on us had become an avenue to showcase our hospitable skills. With the country open to over 20,000 soccer fans across the world, the hotel prepared to cater for dignitaries who had flown from far to witness the tournament. I was still attaché to the presidential castle at the time. Ghana was paired in Group A together with Cameroon, Ivory Coast and Togo. Expectations went high with Kwame Ayew scoring our only goal against Cameroon, giving us a draw. Kwame Ayew again and Otoo Addo scoring the only two goals in the match against our neighbouring Togo and then our humiliating loss against Ivory Coast on 31st January 2000. I believe that was where I stopped following the game altogether. Though originally not a sports fan, I would transform into one whenever my home country was at play. The Super Eagles of Nigeria gave it their all and emerged second after being kicked by Cameroon with a 4-3 on penalties. Their initial euphoria following their qualification to the finals had subsided. Not to dwell on this, but that moment showed me a Ghana I had never seen. My feelings surrounding Afcon 2000 weren't the only "wow" moment that year.

On April 8th 2000, Sarah and I tied the knot. Yes! I fulfilled my promise of bestowing honour upon her and her family. We had courted for a little over two years before going to the altar and our biggest surprise at the time was Sarah's bun in the oven. we were pregnant with our first son Gilbert. We were beyond ourselves with joy when Gilbert Baah Otoo was conceived— He was named in honour of the noblest man I knew, My Grandfather. It was all coming together. my life, my career and my dream family. I got to be the father I've always needed for my son.

Married life was enjoyable for both of us, though we were a young couple with almost nothing to our names. Faith carried us on a daily, and we trusted God to provide always and He did so in many unexpected ways. On some days, I'd beat myself up for being unable to provide my wife with the kind of easy and "soft life" as the millennials termed it. Oh! What I would have given to see her calm and gussied up every day without lifting a finger yet, My Sarah, like me, was a fighter. She'd work tirelessly at the Golden Tulip every day, initiate ways to help us save a portion of our earnings for rainy days and would pray over me on my dark days... I had found a real one. I had spent most of my life seeking approvals and validation from people, but with Sarah, I did not have to try so hard because she saw right through me.

She affectionately bears in mind the happenings of April 4th 2000. It was the day of our Traditional marriage where one of her Uncles walked to the centre of the gathering and spoke these words, "*Abakumah, wo di nipa papa aba fie"*-- Abakumah, you have brought a good man home. *Wei na Obekura abusua no*, this is the man who will keep this family together and bring us glory. One day, if I'm still alive, you will look for me wherever I am to present this stone to Me." This man had never met me, he wasn't present at our knocking ceremony yet, he had approved of me in a heartbeat. Benjamin's takeover of the dance floor was the highlight of my day. Although we disagreed on a few issues, specifically on the subject of his alcoholism, he wasted no time throwing his weight behind me on my big day. It was the perfect form of entertainment, the way he busted interesting moves to *Obrafour's pae mu ka* among other trending hiplife hit songs at the time, kept the guests engaged. He went agog the dance floor. His loud laughs and shouts flowed in harmony with his movements as he continued to keep guests engaged and wanting more of him. He was, without doubt, having the best time of his life. Ben had no girlfriend that I knew of. He had become secretive, even with me. He only liked to crack jokes not share his personal stories. I believe it was the thought to not burden anyone with his issues. He delighted in seeing others laugh, even at his own expense. We couldn't have known the degree of his internal suffering then but today it all makes sense. Kwesi lived out this quote from the late American actor Robin Williams, *"I think the saddest people always try their hardest to make people happy. Because they know what it's like to feel worthless and they do not want anybody else to feel like that."*

Later that month, my wife and I made a collaborative effort to rent a single-room apartment in a compound house two stops away from the Dansoman roundabout. It was a simple cheaply built house which I believe by its appearance was over 2 decades old. My wife and I, excited by the thoughts of beginning a new life together, could care less about the leaky roof and how 'trapping' the room felt. Of course, there were moments I gave myself a hard time for our living conditions yet Sarah assured me that it was no problem when it was. We had proficiently developed ways of tackling the issue of the leaky roof whenever it rained… the 555 stainless buckets and some good old rags! Most typical Ghanaian local landlords are quite unhelpful when it came to maintaining their properties. They were mainly experts in taking their time in counting their advance payment till the last cedi, yet would seldom invest in maintenance. There were other rooms like ours on the same compound, numbering about 10 or perhaps more. We shared a single opened roof bathhouse and a closed toilet facility at the far end of the house. Every morning you'd hear slapping sounds of rubber-made slippers going –to and from the bathhouse while some others aggressively scratched the surface of the cemented compound with the hard bristles of locally made palm brooms as they tidied up the compound, in addition to the ridiculously loud exchange of greetings directly behind the net window while we slept was a daily alert. You've got to love a Ghanaian compound house setting! Everyone poked their noses into anyone's business like there was a total absence of the decency to respect the privacy of others. From the day we first moved in, other co-tenants already had first-hand information on who we were and what we did, yet they walked over to say hello and initiate an introduction. With time, they got acquainted with what time we both left to and from work. Simply put, a Ghanaian compound house was merely an extension of your extended family. Yet, this was an arrangement we had geared up to deal with.

The many efforts Sarah and I made to conceive proved futile though there was the ultimate inner desire to have our DNAs swirl again to create another child of our own, who would be a playmate to both Cecilia and Gilbert, the more we tried, the more reality painted a cruel picture that it wasn't going to happen for us. No matter how hard we tried, our efforts were always rewarded with disappointments. We booked an appointment to see a fertility doctor who had agreed to run several tests on us to determine the cause of the issue. be it hormonal or organ malfunctioning. Turned out, It was all me! The number of years I had spent around heat in the kitchen had finally caught up with me — it had affected the count and quality of my sperm production. As I sat face to face with the doctor and beside my wife with my face downcast, all hopes I had about ever fathering another child had left with the wind. We had both hoped to hear something less shattering, perhaps something like, *"nothing seems to be the problem, the results are clean but we can put you on some medication to speed up the process,"* but instead we were hit with the contrary.

What I loved about Sarah was her level of Faith and resilience in that season of despair. If something seemed amiss, she would step right in with the right words to tilt our perspectives to a positive light. I believe she got that from her mother, the ability to stand still in the wildest storm. Though she was a bit hurt by the outcome of our visit to the doctor, Sarah held on to the counsel given by her mother that in marriage, situations such as these are bound to occur. With counselling and fervent prayer, our several months of trying to conceive were crowned by God's grace. Sarah became once again with child. To the dismay of my wife, I took it upon myself to take charge of all tedious household chores including sweeping and scrubbing the shared compound and bathhouse respectively. It would be a shame to catch her bending or slipping by accident to bring any harm to her or the baby, they were mine to protect. At the 10-tenant occupancy house, the role of keeping the compound and toilet facilities tidy was equally shared exclusively among the female occupants every week. Here, it was required of every woman to take up these duties for 7 whole days before handing over to the next to follow suit. To the males, it was simply preposterous to take up this role so when I did, they passed mindless jokes without a drop of sensitivity to the plight of my wife. Oh, I gave them quite a good laugh!

Sometime in 2002, as the pregnancy progressed, the need to relocate into a much bigger space suddenly dawned on me. We had to make room for the baby and also have some room for privacy ourselves. It was already humiliating to host visitors in our single room where the cheaply acquired locally-made mattress laid. With a quick substantial loan from Madam Hammond, my mother-in-law, we paid and moved into a chamber and hall accommodation at Dansoman Last Stop, about 15 minutes away from where we lived. I knew for a fact that before Sarah allowed her heart to feel anything for me, she had given up a lot; Turning down a rich man among other befitting well-to-do suitors. As we settled into our new home, the urge to step up to my career goals came knocking, I needed to do right by my family.

Back at La Palm, bliss was in the air. I had been promoted to a banquet Chef after the 1999 Ecowas Summit which earned me a bump in my salary. With my new position as a banquet Chef, I was to assist the Executive and Sous Chefs along with overseeing and preparing banquet meals at the hotel's Restaurant. Also attaché to the presidential castle, I continued to cater for all their many banquets and functions.

It was still 2002 and former US president Bill Clinton was expected to visit Ghana on Saturday, September 21st which per records would be Clinton's 2nd official visit to Ghana after he relinquished power in the year 2000. This visit was to see to the launch of his pet project which sought to Build Capital for the Poor. It was a non-governmental organization (NGO) which aimed at mobilizing resources for the poor in the developing world. According to reports from the Statesman Newspaper and Modern Ghana Online that year, Bill Clinton was also expected to sit with Otumfour Osei Tutu II, the Asantehene, among other dignitaries to discuss issues of land and environmental degradation. It was an extremely busy week for the banquet kitchen as we moved all corners to make the stay and nourishment of Bill Clinton one to remember.

He happened to stay at the La Palm Royal Beach Hotel where I was designated as one of the chefs at hand at the time. I prepared a dinner of Spinach (*kontomire*) stew with steamed rice and plantain for him and his entourage. Pleased with the meal, He called to pay his compliments to the chef and enquired about how the meal was prepared. That instantly put me in the spotlight and intrigued the general public to get to know who this young chef was. President Clinton and his team left for La Cote d'Ivoire to launch a similar project after about 2 days if I'm remembering correctly. At La Palm, several opportunities to participate in external cooking competitions were presented. There was the Unilever Maggi competition where I emerged third and the Frytol Unilever competition where I placed first runner-up. Memories from the Frytol competition still stand out to me to this date because of an embarrassing scene I created for myself. Let me briefly address this, as I previously mentioned, I emerged the first runner-up at a Frytol cooking competition which eventually landed me a spot to audition for a Frytol television commercial at the Ghana Broadcasting Corporation (GBC), alongside legendary Ghanaian actor Kofi Adjorlolo. Like a child on Christmas, I got overly excited. Perhaps it was the extreme confidence I had in my ability to perform before the panel. To my surprise, something as uncomplicated as staring into the lens of a camera to recite my well-memorized lines completely crippled and left me anxious... I just couldn't perform. I'd never been the person who dwelled on fear as a reason to not go after what I wanted but I guess I am presently of the belief that that opportunity wasn't mine to keep.

THE NEXT FEW MONTHS continued to put a strain on our finances, my wife and I literally lived from paycheck- to-paycheck in a rented apartment with 2 little mouths who were already eating us out of house and home. To make matters worse, Francis Otoo Jnr. was on the way. We devised a way to stream in some extra income by creating a private extension of what we do best, cooking!

The idea commenced without a proper name or registration. We advertised by word of mouth and grew a handful of clients through positive referrals. We operated and prepared orders from our tiny kitchen mostly on weekends, all the chopping, garnishing, grilling and roasting were carried out from our little home at Dansoman Last stop. Those days were very exhausting. We worked tirelessly to keep the family going. Some nights I'd lay in bed with my eyes staring transfixed at the white washed ceiling with rustling sounds of objects left on compound— there had to be more to my life than this. Moments of my encounter with Bill Clinton came flashing through my mind. it had added an unfeigned sense of worth to my being. I placed myself from the onset of my life right to the place I found myself, laying beside my wife and children. I guess there was a lot to be grateful for after all.

# Chapter 9

# Chapter 9

The Royalhouse Chapel *Ahenfie* sits between Kwame Nkrumah circle and Awudome in Accra-Ghana. The International Bible worship center with over thousands of believers worldwide was founded by the **Apostle General, Rev. Sam Korankye Ankrah** after his encounter with God on June 19, 1991. The Charitable ministry of the chapel continues to spread the gospel and touch many lives of the vulnerable and the neglected in the society.

The Apostle General, in preparation for an annual convention which sought to host people from across the globe, went in search of a chef to cater to the nutritional needs of his guests. So, as he kept reaching out to his connects at various highly rated hotels in the country to recommend a chef who would be up to the task. With almost every hotel he called, I came highly recommended. "Ah there is this guy called Francis at La Palm Royal Beach, you should get in touch with him," they all said. Paying heed to their suggestion, he phoned someone at La palm to enquire of this young chef Francis everyone sung about. "Could you please get him to the phone? I would like to speak to him." He pleaded. Hear my truth, though I had called on God and his servants in my days of despair at Ho Polytechnic, I, however, continued to harbor some skepticism about some men of God…if not most. When I was informed that it was the Apostle at the other end of the receiver, I wondered what he wanted. I instantly recalled a time he came over to the hotel with his other ministers in tow for a fellowship. They looked quite young at the time, perhaps in their mid to late thirties. The wait staff at the hotel was beyond excited.

Whispers went round about the Apostle's visit to the Hotel, "Rev Sam Korankye Ankrah, the man of God who preaches on radio on Mondays is here o!" I looked on with an impassive face. "*tweaa* these men of God are swindlers, Always manipulating people by spreading falsehood as prophecies to milk them dry." I derived no pleasure in being in their presence. I however went to the phone to hear him out as a sign of courtesy.

"Hello sir," I started.
"Hello Chef Francis, how are you doing?"
"I'm fine thank you."
"Right. I would like to schedule for an appointment to have a discussion with you."
"Sure. Kindly let me know the time and venue and I'll be there."
Sarah was not new to my raging perceptions about men of God. So, when I got home that evening, I narrated what had occurred and elaborated on my hidden intention to hit him with a ridiculous charge for my services.

I lamented, "Look at these small small men of God o. He wants me to come and cook and take care of his guests."
"And what's wrong with that?" Sarah questioned.
"Hwɛ, I will charge him *bia* he will never forget." I had decided to raise my charge to have him change his mind about ever working with me again.
"How about you go and hear him out. Just go for a trial and let's see how things unfold from there," she advised.
As always, considering my wife's wise words, I honored the Apostle's invitation to discuss catering for his visiting guests throughout the span of the conference. I made mention of my 'high' rate to which he replied, "No problem." Every morning I would show up at the residence of the Apostle, sharply dressed and ready to cook up a storm of the requested menu. I would serve the guests, clear up my workspace and march out to La Palm for my shift. The next day was no different.

I conducted my duties with such swiftness that the Apostle found it bizarre. "*ei* is this one a ghost?" he asked the butler. "I can't seem to comprehend his work ethics. No no...this guy is too smart on the job for my liking." He continued amidst laughter. He appeared impressed by my services and looked forward to seeing me the next day. I showed up the next day with my wife to wrap up the job and to receive my idea of a 'ridiculous charge.'

My wife and I after successfully catering for the guests walked to say hello to the Apostle General. Following the exchange of pleasantries, He drew closer to me and uttered the very words that planted me on the path to becoming this chef you're intrigued to learn more about.

He began, "I know we spoke about money but I am going to give you something more than that." My eyes widened. My naivety triggered a thought, 'what on earth could be worth more than money?'

He continued with an authoritative command over every word that came forth from his mouth as I stood perplexed before him at the entrance of the kitchen, "I am going to release you into your future and destiny." He instructed me to kneel down and fired away with the word of God and with prayers into my life.

*"You will be travelling out of this nation as an International Chef. I have released the blessings of God upon you. The door is open, the heavens are open. That offer would present avenues to serve and cater for Presidents, Royals and notable men and women of Power, which would stir up a reaction of change in your life and that of your family's destiny in three months."* We responded with an "Amen" with Sarah's being the loudest. If I'm being honest, I personally contended with the word I received though my eyes were filled with tears. At this point you could call me a doubting Thomas because my faith at the time was still at infancy, making me contend with divinity from a human

understanding. While a part of me embraced this as a mere spoken word, the other part listened with some hope that it could indeed manifest. I needed to see this to truly believe… I silently dared God in my heart. He held out an envelope containing the payment we had both agreed on, and flashed us a smile as we turned towards the exit.

Of course, every word of prophecy spoken by the Apostle still came a bit off to me. Don't get me wrong, though young in faith, I, still, reverenced the anointing on the Man of God. Like the typical Ghanaian man, I was simply not the type to be bowled over by prophecies especially given the number of false Prophets who had risen mightily in my days. They were, again, notorious for communicating their self serving "messages from God" aimed at amassing followers and enriching their accounts, I had no delight in becoming yet another unwitting prey. As already stated earlier, though the situation I had found myself in back at Ho Poly led me to call on the support of Men of God for a prayer of redemption, it had nothing to do with prophecies. I Guess I was more of the *'Go to church, say a prayer and God will provide what is yours'* kind of a believer. Meanwhile, standing in the presence of the Apostle, I had said my 'Amens' with a heart full of uncertainty and made my way back home. "Have a little more faith in the man of God and live with some expectancy," Sarah advised when I raised the issue on the prophecy given. "Three months dear, in three months, I would be offered an opportunity out of this country which would mark a new beginning for us? Ha! How do you expect me to believe this dear? Who on earth could turn out to be that generous?" On my mental list, I had already crossed out names of members of my extended family abroad because, the onetime I had expressed any interest going overseas was to my dear old Ma, who clearly ruled out soliciting help from my uncles abroad because we were of the awareness that they would not be willing to help in anyway. I had since come to make my peace with never going beyond the shores of Africa but my wife, on other hand, made room for doubts. She held on to the word and rode on with it. Settling into the two-seater sofa in the living room, I pulled out the envelope handed over by the Apostle to cross check and record in our foolscap notebook. Where we kept account of whatever external profits or loses accrued from our catering business. Perhaps I was under an illusion. I counted over the notes and handed them to Sarah to confirm the amount contained in the envelope. We had received 4 to 5 times more than I had bargained. He tells me, that he thought I had charged way below the worth of the services I had rendered at his residence. He felt that my professionalism deserved more reward than what I had charged. I said to my wife, "wow, I wasn't expecting the man of God to be this generous." From across the room, Sarah replied, standing with her arms resting on her hips, "you see? I told to just go give him a try, and here you are already with an unexpected testimony *afei s*j *w'ani awu,* you're ashamed." Her laughter was one of excitement, clad with a sense of gratitude. Still, like the typical partial believer I was, I made a conscious effort to not sugarcoat my words or cave in to Sarah's opinion. So I replied, "Look, this man *paaa*, he merely uttered those big big things and added this gift only because, I had done a good job for him and he wants me to come back." I threw in a chuckle and headed out to the bathroom to freshen up for the night. The gift, the prophecy, everything the Apostle had exhibited had honestly stuck with me from that evening till this day. The Apostle had somehow captured my heart. That night, I lay in bed with some sort of excitement and if I'm being honest, some degree of embarrassment because he had singlehandedly debunked the earlier prejudice I had pushed regarding the likes of him. As I drifted off to sleep, scenes from the encounter flooded my mind. There was, however, one thing to look forward to... the manifestation of the prophecy.

I woke up the next morning to prepare to go about business as usual. Get to La Palm, do what I loved and was good at, get home to my family and repeat till the weekdays were exhausted without the luxury of leisure. The subsequent weeks weren't any different. I got busy shifting every minute into my role as a banquet chef as I had a lot to tend to.

Seemed like a perfect space for a chef of my caliber to fully settle and operate until that fateful Wednesday when a mysterious lady walked up to me. She was slim, had dark skin and average in height. She had walked into the establishment seeking specifically for an audience with me.

"Hello Chef Francis, I'm Patricia." She started with her right hand extended as a gesture for a handshake.

"Hello Patricia" I responded firmly grabbing her hand, "Pleased to meet you, to what do I owe this visit?"

"Well, I have an event coming up in one of the neighboring African countries and would love to engage your services throughout the entire week of the occasion."

I couldn't have known it then, but this offer would come to change the trajectory of the life I had come to settle for. I posed the necessary questions: the number of expected guests, the variety of meals on the menu and all. Judging by her appearance, I didn't quite peg her as capable enough to afford my services for the kind of event she greatly described. If there was a word beyond "simple," I think that's how she appeared to me. Perhaps too simple to even grace the halls of La Palm. She dialed my number on her phone so she'd remember to save it later to keep in touch. Still struck by her demeanor, I thought it bizarre for a stranger as she, to walk up to me with such an offer. It briefly weighed heavily on my mind till I swept under the carpet to proceed with what was left of my hours. Of course I discussed it with Sarah, we shared everything. It was just too much of a big deal to keep it away from her. Sarah was quite skeptical of the offer and so was I. with reason being that, Ghana was already in a state of panic as rumors of *juju* practitioners, robbing men of their penises with just a tap on the shoulder had spread like wildfire. To that extent of our lives, we have had enough physical struggles and were in no hurry to accumulate a spiritual one on top of matters. Together, we informed the Apostle General Rev. Sam Korankye Ankrah over the phone, who nudged me to follow through with it.

With a brand new inspiration in the absence of the previous underlying fears and perceptions, I agreed to meet up with Patricia at Achimota, precisely the area between Mile 7 and Kingsby roundabout for final discussions on the trip the so-called African country.

"Do you own a passport?" She asked.

"Nope" I replied with some loss of face

"Not to worry, I'll call for your details later to complete the proceedings once my partners confirm your budget."

"Sure, thank you madam. I'll take my leave now."

Having initially proclaimed the offer as an elaborate hoax, I suddenly became fascinated by every minutiae of the future event. Squeezing into the passengers' seat of the red and yellow taxi, my brain drowned into a series of storylines where I executed my task with a signature of class and professionalism. I imagined strangers coming in to pay their compliments to the chef and acknowledging the exquisite taste of the meals... it gave me something to look forward to.

Patricia took vivid directions to my Dansoman home. She needed that and some additional information for the bio data page of the passport she was processing on my behalf. It was about quarter to 8pm when a startling Knock on the plywood trap door of our chamber and hall apartment threw my heavily pregnant wife into a panic. I stepped out to meet a group of men in suits like in a James Bond movie with matching dark sunglasses, mean mugging like they can't smile. They asked if I was Francis Otoo to which I responded in the affirmative in a clear steady voice. as the man of the house, I could not afford to give away my fears in a quavering tone. They handed over a brown envelope and turned to the exit. My wife after spying through the net windows, burst into loud wails, "Joojo what have you done? Who have you gotten yourself involved with? Joojo we have children ooo *erh!* Please what's going on?" She was frantic with concerns for our safety and I wish I had answers to calm her nerves in the moment. I still held the brown envelope, gutless to tear it open. When I finally did, I had the shock of my life. It was a passport, my passport and in it was a 5 year diplomatic Visa to the United States of America, I was in disbelief. Patricia called two minutes later to reveal that, all conversations held in regards to the job offer, was an interview in disguise. The real offer was to work as the private chef to **Ghana's Ambassador to the United States** at the time, in the person of **Honorable Alan Kojo Kyeremateng**, her husband. My joy knew no bounds. The only downside was that, we were to leave the shores of Ghana in seven days to begin this new role. Sarah instantly became visibly sick when I broke the news to her. It was the idea of being apart after years of no separation whatsoever. The pregnancy hormones worsened her plight. She constantly worried of our being apart from eachother indefinitely among other pestering thoughts she failed to audibly voice out in her sorrowful state. *"It's always been the two of us. It's always been us both of us against the world Francis, how am I going to cope without you?"* she questioned sadly.

My mother in-law was the best figure to involve in our nerve-wracking situation. She had agreed to have Sarah come live with her for a few days to calm her down. She opened Sarah up to the possibilities of securing of a better future for herself and our kids if she allowed me to pursue the offer a lifetime. It was tough, but she had come to accept that it was necessary for me to leave. Upon her return back home, Sarah drew my attention to the prophecy given exactly 3 months ago by the Apostle General. I could not believe it. There I was with my very eyes watching the words I gracefully doubted unfolding right before me. God is indeed good!

She said to me, "This is a divine opportunity of a life time for you and it'll be selfish on my part to be a hindrance. This is a clear manifestation of God's prophetic plan for your life and today, I stand in agreement with it." Whatever counsel my mother in-law gave my wife to warrant these wifey words of approval definitely made a difference in our preparations towards the given date of departure. Quick rounds were made to Kantamanto. The hub for second hand clothing in Ghana where I purchased what I was convinced could defend me from the cold weather in America.

1st March 2003, with about 2 months left for Francis Otoo Jnr. To be delivered, I arrived together with my wife, My Mum and mother in-law at the Kotoka International Airport, where I was to depart with **Mrs Patricia Kyeremateng** to the United States. My wife had given her approval for me to leave, yet her demeanor seemed otherwise. There are no words to describe the severity of the heartache we both felt at the final moments. Our good-byes felt like it was forever, yet it wasn't. A sudden concern about how my wife was going to cope with the pressures of delivery and the raising of our two older kids by herself worried me to a great extent. Had I not thought it all through like I assumed? What if things did not go as planned? Leaving my family behind was nerve wracking, yet a part of me knew that embarking on this journey was for the greater good.

There I was at the Airport, still shaken to my bones as I walked right into an unfolding Prophecy. The words of the Apostle General, spoken over my life at the kitchen door of his private residence that fateful evening had truly activated the words of God over my life. I had indeed been released into the office of an international chef divinely orchestrated by the power of God…An unexpected means to a new beginning.

# Chapter 10

# Chapter 10

Nevertheless, the concept of Prophets, Prophecy and Faith was quite lost on me till I recently sat side-by-side Reverend Sam Korankye Ankrah to gain a more accurate understanding on the aforementioned trio. In the exclusive discussion I freely share with you below to aid your comprehension on the subjects, he elaborates on the individuality of each concept and how they work in concert with one another.

**The place of a prophet, the Mystery of Faith and Prophecy In the words of the Apostle General:**

I will raise them up a prophet from among their brethren, like unto thee, and will put my words in his mouth. And he shall speak unto them all that I shall command him. And it shall come to pass, that whosoever will not hearken unto my words which he shall speak in my name, I will require it of him.
Deuteronomy 18:18-19, KJV.

Why would God hold man accountable? Because the prophet represents the voice of God. The prophet is the medium through which the mind of god concerning his people is communicated. So, when a man adheres to the instructions of the true prophet of God, he has accepted the commands or directions of God. He said, he who does not listen to him, in reference to the prophet, I will take to account.

The place of a prophet is essential to the life of a man because like I stated initially, He is the vessel through which God communicates and directs mankind. It says in Amos 3:7, surely the lord will do nothing, but he revealeth his secret unto his servants the prophets. Under the Old Testament, the prophet speaks for God, under the New Testament, when Jesus Christ came to surrender on the cross for mankind. God released His Holy Spirit to permanently abide with us. So now, the Holy Spirit has taken the place of the Old Testament prophets, who mostly delivered warnings from God whenever his people were going astray, to minister unto us. The New Testament prophets point people to Christ as means of Salvation. To let people know that Jesus Christ is the way, the truth and the light. Nevertheless, there are still mouthpieces this day that are genuinely used by the Holy Spirit to communicate the mind of God like in the days of old. And then follows the question of how to discern between a true prophet of god and a false prophet. 1 john 4:1 provides a vivid guidance on doing so. The apostle john admonishes us to believe not every spirit, but try the spirits whether they are of god: because many false prophets are gone out into the world. This is where he differentiates between the two kinds of prophets, from the second to the third verse he says, hereby know ye the spirit of god: every spirit that confesseth that Jesus Christ is come in the flesh is of God: and every spirit that confesseth not that Jesus Christ is come in the flesh is not of God: and this is that spirit of antichrist, whereof ye have heard that is should come. And even now already is it in the world. Sadly, in our day and age, there many existing false prophets who are parading the streets in the name of Christ misleading people. Precisely as there is a way to test the originality of your phone or even your toothpaste, there is a way to test the authenticity of a prophecy from a prophet.

First, the prophecy must confirm the word of God. If the message from the man is in conflict with the word of God, it is simply not of God. For instance, a man walks up to you to a word 'supposedly' from God and says, "Prepare to divorce your wife for God is bringing you a new wife." Reject that prophecy because it contradicts the word of God in Mark 10:9 that what therefore God hath joined together, let not man put asunder. So if God has given you a wife in Holy matrimony, why would this same God go against his command and ask you put your wife aside for another one. That prophet is just misleading you. If one, however, commits to that prophecy, he will discover that the same issue experienced with the previous spouse will recur. If he decides to move on to another, the same issue will follow onto the next. Should he commit to the very first marriage and makes the conscious effort to tackle the basic problem of temperament, uncompromising attitudes, understanding etc. he will realize the need to not pay heed to the prophecy of divorce.

Additionally, one can test prophecy with the character of the man of God. God will not use vessels who unremorsefully and constantly defile their bodies with adultery and fornication. Before you pay heed to the prophecy being spoken, it is advisable to check the background of the vessel in communication with you.

Brethren, be not deceived, for there are a lot of falsehood being peddled all over the place. Some of these men speak from their minds rather than from God to mostly serve themselves. They go about making declarations for God when He has said nothing. But when a true prophet is being used of God, he speaks and there are results. The receiver of His word enjoys the blessings of God in peace and in liberty. Even when there are trials, it is short-lived because, God sends help always in the nick of time. Hope in Him maketh not ashamed. Prophecies from self serving prophets can equally manifest, why? Because, it is a directive from the agents of the enemy to lead into a life contrary to the mind of God for your life. It will lead you into trials, danger and overwhelming difficulties. He may carry a Bible yet, it is however necessary to test all spirits like Apostle John said so as to not be trapped in the whims of the enemy.

Moreover, regardless of how genuine a prophet may be, a prophecy may be hindered when one fails to apply faith. **Faith** is fundamental to the works of divinity. In the absence of it, one simply cannot key into the works or the promises of God. Hebrews 11:1 defines faith as the substance of things hoped for, the evidence of things not seen. So what Francis, what you did in your case was that, though you deemed yourself a partial believer, you dared God in your heart because you saw him faithful or capable enough to fulfill what he had said, hence its manifestation. Hebrews 11:6 goes ahead to say, But without faith it is impossible to please Him: for he that cometh to God must believe that he is, and that He is a rewarder of them that diligently seek Him. How do you seek God? Through his word, through prayer, through fellowship with the Holy Spirit. it is faith that unravels, reveals or unveils the things that you need to know about God and to receive of God. So, When Abraham received the prophecy that how would have a child, he and Sarah, questioned The Authenticity of the prophecy in comparison to their physical condition. It was a preposterous word to be taken seriously, how can a 100 year old man with erectile dysfunction and a 90 year old woman with a dead womb and had gone the menopausal stage have a child? In the realms of logic, science, the prophecy was an outright nonsense. Biology would not support conception for persons at that age.

But hear this. There is a contention between the 'human impossibility' with what I call the 'divine impossibility.' Divine impossibility is where the one who has spoken is called Jehovah Elohim, Adonai, The God who does all things and with him all things are possible. He is the one who is saying, yes you are 100 but you are going to produce a child, yes you are 90 and have gone past menopause but you are going to conceive and carry a full-term pregnancy and have a safe delivery. So now, science is fighting the word of God, and Humanity, which is also reality, is fighting divinity which you, however, have the choice to accept only based on faith. At this juncture, what will bring the prophecy to manifestation? Nothing but Faith. Abraham embraced it, at that point I believe He said, "you know what? My body is telling me that I can't have a child. When I look at my wife, with all her fallen teeth, I do not know how we will be able to bring forth this child." so I'll go to Romans 4:20, He staggered not at the promise of God through unbelief, but was strong in faith, giving glory to God. It implied that against all odds, he believed God unto him who can accomplish all things. And the Bible said that it was counted to him for righteousness. When God saw that Abraham believed, he rewarded and honoured his righteousness. So, in Genesis 18:10-12, when God was speaking the promise through the three passing men to Abraham in the plains of mamre, that he should tell his wife that according to the time of life, he shall certainly return unto them and Sarah would bear a son, Sarah laughed. Yet in Chapter 21, Sarah had delivered the baby and she begins with an exclamation, "eii who would have thought that at the age of 90, I will bear a son, for now, all who hear this will call me blessed. They will laugh with me. I will call him Isaac because God has put laughter in my mouth." What happened there? The prophecy had come to pass because a man chose to believe in divinity as against the suggestions of human feelings.

Like faithlessness, doubt and disobedience can hinder the manifestation of prophecy. Some prophecies may come with divine instructions. So as a sign of belief, one must obey the instructions that may come with a prophecy. For instance,

Naaman's miracle in 2 kings 5:9-14 was tied to his obedience to prophetic instructions given by Elisha. As long as he fumed at the direction and did not wash in the Jordan River, the miracle wasn't happening until his little servant spoke unto him saying, "Papa, you've travelled to Israel and the prophet did not ask anything untoward. He's only asked you to bathe in the river and you will be healed. If you comply and nothing happens, praise God, if something happens, To God be the glory." I'm sure Naaman was a bit hesitant in his response though he had listened to his servant. "Okay, okay," he said, and dipped himself in the river. 1, 2 …7 times and the leprosy was gone! His flesh came again like that of a little child. Naaman became whole not because Elisha had prophesied, but because he had obeyed the instruction that came with the prophecy, hence its manifestation. You must also Love the God who has sent forth His word to you. Most people believe that, the reason to why their expected breakthroughs or miracles have been delayed is because God despises them. God does not and cannot despise his own creation. You are the work of his mighty hands, uniquely and wonderfully made. God has not delayed your miracle because he wants to punish you, no, God has been preparing you so that when the miracle manifests, you will be well equipped to handle it. At times, the delay of our miracle could also be God's protection from an impending danger. We have a lot of people praying for wealth without necessarily having the wisdom to handle the depths of it. God is saying, "Son, I will bless you with wealth but you are yet to come to the understanding that, money is to help society, my work and my people so let me groom you a little bit. When you come to that place of understanding, I will bless you with more than you have prayed for." So, that delay does not imply that God has forsaken you, That delay might be to save you so that the miracle you have been praying so hard for, does not run you into trials and temptations or at worst, kill you. Ignorance, Unpreparedness are also clear factors that can hinder the manifestation of prophecy. To cap it all, Faithlessness, lack of preparation, disobedience to adhere prophetic instructions, doubts, No love for God and for the reason behind the release of the blessing and even sin are factors that can greatly impede the manifestation of prophecy. As a side note, it is important to remember that, God is a merciful God, even when we miss out on our prophecies with sin, he avails unto us second chances to get it right. If for some reason, the prophecy was cut off somewhere in the middle, because we missed out on the purpose of its manifestation due to lack of obedience, sin, faithlessness, lack of preparation, whatever be the reason for the hindrance. God will always give you another chance to make it right. The bible says in Proverbs 24:16, for a just man falleth seven times and riseth up again: but the wicked shall fall into mischief. If we come up to him, He will not turn us away. As many times as we ask Him for forgiveness, He's always willing and just to forgive us and heal us from our trespasses. He's a God of second chances. When we miss it, He will give us another chance. However, the only caution is to not take the liberty to constantly repeat the same mistake which drew us away from the manifestation of the prophecy. When one keeps deliberately taking advantage of the grace and mercies of god and indulges in things which draw him away from the presence of God, He is likened to a fool.

*Golden Tulip Hotel, where it all started... this place gave me everything; from finding my identity, my voice, my confidence and the love of my life.*

*Every whip, every chop and set up, represents an individual's creativity, a chef knowledge and desire to give out the best of what he possesses, his skill.*

*La- Palm Royal beach Hotel, my first walk through its doors in 1999, marked the beginning of greatness, God's plan to honor and favor me unfolded before my very eyes.*

*The Ghanaian village restaurant, located at the La-Palm Royal beach hotel.*

*The front view of the Ghanaian village restaurant.*

*The thatch roof, the hut-style buildings, truly defining what the restaurant represents... a typical Ghanaian village.*

*As one of the pioneers of the Ghanaian Village Restaurant, I stare at these photos with a lot of pride. After almost two decades since its establishment, it is indeed refreshing to see the restaurant thriving with what it does best... serving all guests with authentic Ghanaian delicacies.*

*Away from the kitchen, working at the La-Palm was quite therapeutic. Access to the ocean beyond the green lawns and coconut gardens gave me all the breather I needed to feel refreshed and revitalized after my shift hours.*

*This photograph isn't doing justice enough to reveal the Greek-style pool at the La-Palm. At least, you could tell from the mini-bridge over the pool that, it is in fact massive; beginning right from the back doors of the reception to the edge of the coconut gardens.*

*My moment with the late former President Jerry John Rawlings! The most down-to-earth yet firm man I had ever met. This was in 1999, during my time at as a chef attaché the Osu castle.*

*This! ...The defining moment of my career and first step to culinary stardom. These were Pleasant moments after I had prepared and served former President Bill Clinton of America with ampesi and spinach/ kontomire stew.*

*With my Papa, The Apostle General Rev. Sam Korankye Ankrah, I have shared a lot of memories. This was one of those times in Israel.*

*The look on my face says it all; this was the day I made the best decision of my life. To walk my Abakumah to the altar was the day I earned favor in the eyes of God. I found a wife and a good thing*

*Upon this very ground, I knelt before the Lord; on this very ground the Spirit of God ministered unto me through his servant, Apostle General Rev. Sam Korankye Ankrah, at his private residence. On this small square area before his kitchen, I received word on the plans of God for my life, which continues to manifest even till this day.*

*The vessel of God through my faith was built and the course of my life defined, Apostle General Reverend Sam Korankye Ankrah, founder of Royal house chapel, Ahenfie.*

*Hon. Alan Kyeremateng, the current trade minister of Ghana and a former ambassador to the USA, pictured with his wife, Mrs. Patricia Christabel Kyeremateng.*

# Part 3

# New Beginnings

# Chapter 11

# Chapter 11

It turned out my idea of a winter jacket was actually a spring jacket, certainly not designed to ward off the piercing colds of America. Nothing could have prepared me for the numbing breeze which slapped my face as we emerged from the plane. We boarded a KLM flight from Ghana through Amsterdam Schipol Airport in transit to Dulles International Airport (IAD), Virginia. "Are we really in America?" I asked Frank Ameho in disbelief after successfully going through immigration, He was a butler also employed by Mrs Kyeremateng to help manage the residence of the Ambassador. As we exited the main Airport building towards the car park, Hon. Alan Kyeremateng waited with some dignitaries in a car to receive us.

The scenery surrounding the gigantic Airport building as we drove past it was picturesque, gaining beauty from the clear colouring of the blue and grey skies. It looked as if I was copied and pasted into a perfect photograph. There I was, the lowly boy from South Labadi Estates huddled together in a car with notable dignitaries. Enjoying the views from the window. watching building after building sitting in heaps of snow, it finally echoed through my mind that I was truly in the United States. In about 45 minutes, we arrived at the Potomac Residence of the Ambassador in Maryland. My eyes widened in a new wonder as my ankles got buried in snow in front of the beautiful mansion. It became apparent that this was going to be my place of abode. The sprint jacket gave me away to the cold as my body broke into strong shivers. We got the luggage out of the vehicle into the house where Mrs Kyeremateng showed Frank and me our separate quarters. it was still morning. By evening I had settled into my new home ready to begin life anew in another man's land. Before that, Mrs Kyeremateng had shown us around the residence and to my workstation, the kitchen, to familiarize myself. The kitchen was spectacular. It had enough room for me to swing my arm-wielding pots and pans from one end to the other to create delicacies of all kinds. My passion for cooking had carried me that far by the Grace of God hence there was no room to tolerate mistakes. I took in a deep breath. Yes, this is America!

As the new resident chef, I had to develop and plan menus and daily specials to suit my employers. I managed food costing and inventory and maintained standards for food storage, quality and appearance on a daily. The food on the menu was a complete stir of authentic Ghanaian dishes and a variety of continental dishes. I recall s*hrimp gari fortor* being the first meal I prepared for Hon. Alan Kyeremateng, which instantly became his personal favourite. Growing up in South Labadi Estates with my late grandmother gave me the avenue to experiment with some of the gari she made my brother and I hawk on the streets. I discovered as a young boy that, one could do more with it than just soak it in a bowl of chilled water together with a spoon of sugar, powdered milk and peanuts to enjoy as a homemade cereal. I mastered the art of making authentic j*ba*, gari *fortor* and gari biscuits etc.

**Shrimp Gari** *fortor* is the elite luxurious version of the original gari *fortor* which requires extra flavouring and garnish of the sauce to determine the taste of the final dish. With this dish, it is always important to allow the sauce to cool before you add the gari, or else the hot sauce could end up giving the gari a starchy texture and appearance. a doughy consistency instead of a crumbly one is considered a total fail. Gari fortor is popular in Ghana, West Africa and across Ghanaian communities across

the world. It is quick to prepare and quite easy on the stomach. Here! Let's pause as I walk you through how to prepare simple Gari *fortor*. To start with, you'll need: 200g Gari 60 ml warm water (with little salt added if desired) 60 ml cooking oil 1-2 peeled and finely chopped onions 2-3 chopped ripe tomatoes 1-5 green chilies dash of garlic dash of smoked paprika, basil, coriander leaves, ground anise Maggi stock cube tomato paste 2 beaten eggs 1 unbeaten egg salt to taste 1 lb seasoned shrimp
To begin.

- Put gari in a bowl and sprinkle a little water to moisten. Stir to get the moisture evenly spread in the gari.
- Chop Onions and tomatoes
- Fry onions and tomatoes, and add tomato paste in a heated pan on medium to high heat for about 5 minutes until onions tenderize.
- Add spices to taste (smoked paprika, chilli pepper, garlic, basil, Maggi cube and coriander leaves).
- Boil unbeaten egg separately and sauté your seasoned shrimp on the side.
- Add 2 beaten eggs to onion and tomato stew and stir as you would to scrambled eggs.
- Add moistened gari to the egg stew
- Remove from heat to serve.
- Add boiled eggs and shrimp to gari fortor to complete the assignment!

Voila! Your meal is served. Give your taste buds a treat as you enjoy your gari *fortor* along with your choice of protein and a side of your favourite beverage. You're welcome! Let's save my recipe for the super luxurious Shrimp gari *fortor* among other local and continental recipes for my cookbook.

About 2 months into my job, my wife back home in Ghana was due to deliver our second son, Francis Otoo Jnr on 4th May 2003. Under the mercies of God, both mother and child were healthy and had developed zero complications until the next day. Junior developed a slight increase in body temperature and cried throughout the night into the 3rd and 4th days. Troubled, Sarah called for the attention of a nurse who told her it was normal for some newborns to cry for several days after being delivered. My wife shared a ward at the private hospital with a new mother who constantly aired her suspicions and concerns about Junior's condition as his temperature kept rising by the hour. The doctors came in later to administer some medications but to no avail, Junior's condition only worsened. Thereafter, He was transferred to receive emergency care at the Korle Bu Teaching Hospital. I was alarmed when the call came through. My wife spoke in a manner I had never heard before.

"It's been 3 days since your son was delivered, and he wouldn't stop crying. We are quite frightened by his rising temperature so Ruby and my mum are going with us to Korle Bu."

Without hesitation, I called on the Apostle General Rev. Sam Korankye Ankrah to deliver the news. In as much as my son was going to receive medical care, it is the Lord who exercises the healing power. Rev Sam almost immediately organized some leaders of the church to pray for our son. Now considered a part of his family and spiritual son, the Apostle General wasted no time in stepping in together with his wife and his team of prayer warriors to intercede on behalf of my family. They battled and prevailed in prayer against whichever spirit wanted to snuff out the life of my little boy. Where they needed to support financially, they did generously. I guess it was what was expected of Spiritual parents but more importantly, they did that because they wanted to rescue the future of my nearly week-old son, who, today, is commanding academic exploits in an Ivy League school in America. I see why God intervened the way He did.

Some minutes later, Sarah received a call from a lady who worked as a nurse at Korle Bu. It appeared that she was off duty that evening and was not to return to work till after 48 hours but because of our relationship with Rev. Sam, she was willing to show up early the next morning to attend to our son, to also ensure that they were well taken care of and was given a good ward. Mama Rita, Rev Sam's wife, was not left out of my call log. Neither were my mum and Sarah's uncle... I got all hands on board to work towards keeping my son alive and healthy. My calls were rampant, and being miles away from my family at that moment made me uneasy. I simply wasn't ready to lose a son— a newborn I was yet to meet and shower with kisses. In a bid to have me get a hold of myself, Sarah communicated exactly what she thought I needed to hear. That Jnr was in a stable condition. After running several tests, the Doctors came in later that night to deliver rather unfortunate news. My son was in a dire situation and could not be discharged. He had to be placed in the ICU because he had contracted jaundice and for a child that young, it was most likely he might not survive.

"No not me, my son will survive. He will live to bury me one day, not the other way." Sarah retorted.

Junior was immediately separated from his mother and placed in an incubator to undergo conventional phototherapy treatment. The therapy was performed with special fluorescent brightness from bili light lamps, emitting blue rays, which shone directly on my baby's skin. His eyes were protected with the aid of paper-like eye wear strapped gently across both little eyes. It was heartbreaking that a child had to be subjected to all this as a "welcome to earth." The treatment, I came to understand, was the most infallible way to treat jaundice in newborns. Sarah was forced to go home without her newborn and return the next day clinging to hopes that he'd survive the night. There was a feeling of needing to be present at the hospital with my family. I initiated talks with my employers to give me a few days off work to attend to matters at home and was literally on the verge of booking the next available flight to Ghana yet my wife advised that it was quite early in my new job to make such demands and questioned exactly what I was going to do to speed up our son's recovery. She had a point, was my presence going to magically reduce the bilirubin build-up in my son's body and flush out the disease from his body? No. the only and most important thing I could bring myself to do was to keep on praying to God to turn the situation around. I was helpless.

Every morning, Sarah would arrive at the hospital at 6 am with my mother-in-law to wait at the doors of the ICU till they were open to allow mothers to see their children. In those gut-wrenching moments, one had to hope that his or her child would be counted amongst the living. While everything happened, my late brother, who at this point had become buddies with Sarah, would call in to check on her and to find out how junior fared. As a show of support, he would say something like, *"In Joojo's absence, I am Junior's father now. I may be financially incapable to assist but please, when you need a shoulder, just know that you can have mine."* There were days Sarah would hear and see mothers wail after the doors were open. It seemed almost rotational, one kid dying after the other. Mothers wailed for the loss of their newborns who had suffered the same ailment as Junior. The scene became a morning routine. Almost something Sarah looked forward to every day— hours of facing various levels of anxiety until she'd lay eyes on our son to be convinced that he survived the night. Those days were dark.

On one such day as the doors flung open, Sarah rushed to our

son's crib amidst the wails of despair from other mothers only to find his crib empty. Oh my God! Her legs melted to the floor followed by a burst of tears. She could not believe it. Every grain of hope she had held on to dashed out the door. As she lay on the floor rolling in her misery while being restrained by her mother, two nurses approached to probe what the issue was.
She answered, "I came to see my son, but he's not here. Please tell me where they took his body. Please, please help me" touched by her sad state, the nurses proceeded to take the details of our son to help them find where his body had been kept. "Paa Kwesi, Francis Junior?" the second nurse repeated after Sarah. "Oh, madam your son is alive. We just switched his room because one of the babies cried all night and disturbed his sleep. Besides, his condition has improved so the doctor approved to switch his room." Sarah quickly wiped her face and hurried off the floor. "Please take me to him," she said reaching for the nurse's hand. Immediately she set eyes on our son lying peacefully in his crib, with tears in her eyes she gave him a long embrace. Mrs Rita Korankye Ankrah went over to pray over Junior on Friday. In her words, she prophesied that Junior will be declared jaundice free and will be discharged on Sunday. Well, who am I to contend with the word of God? At that point, I believed all she uttered because the prophecy given to me by her husband concerning my departure to serve dignitaries in a foreign land had come to pass at the exact appointed time. so, We took the word and run with it. It was highly unorthodox for one to be discharged from the hospital on a Sunday yet, true to Mama Rita's words. Junior was declared jaundice free and was discharged from the hospital after spending almost a month on admission. Today my little boy is almost 18 years old and a freshman at the University of Maryland, USA.
**6 months** into my new job, I lived every minute of my time fully immersed in a cycle of the ever-evolving tastes in the meals

requested by my new employers and all dignified guests who walked through the gates of the residency. I had already been pressed to keep up with their sophistication to tailor their needs and expectations to every dish I created. As I finally allowed myself to settle into this space after a roller coaster of emotions derived from Junior's ailment, a bombshell was dropped. The Ambassador, Hon. Alan Kyeremateng was recalled by Former President Kuffour to return to Ghana. I believe that it was to hone his abilities for Presidential candidacy.

He called Frank and me together for a meeting to discuss the issue at hand. There was a deep honesty in the manner he rendered his regrets. He emphasized how it was unfortunate that he untimely ended our careers back home in Ghana to only drag us into an unfortunate situation. He said, "You gentlemen have been of an enormous help to us and I am open to taking you back to Ghana to continue working with me if only you're willing to." However, there was the readiness to provide accommodation and to ensure that we were taken care of if we ended up concluding on staying back in the United States. I began contemplating. It's been a little over 6 months in the USA and my job at hand is already gone. I did not doubt that the ambassador could help us secure a new or even better job in Ghana, yet a part of me was challenged to test the waters in "another man's land." It would only be fair to see how I'd fare in America. if God forbid things go south, I could always return home to Ghana. Frank Ameho, the butler, also agreed on staying back in America for a new beginning. The change was going to be uncomfortable, yet I imagined it as a necessity for growth.

By the end of 2003, Hon. Alan Kyeremateng and his chain of dignified appointees had responded to the call of the president to return home to assume office as a Minister of Trade, Industry, Private Sector Development (PSD) and the Presidential Special Initiative (PSI). Frank and I continued to stay at the Potomac residence and remained on the embassy's payroll. The former Ambassador had truly kept his promise. Processes to secure my wife a visa were in the pipeline and with Alan gone, it grew quite difficult to finalize the task. Each day came with its own stories surrounding why the visa had been delayed with fresh demands for some extra documentation and details about my wife etc. just tiresome! I held on to an assurance that my wife will be issued a visa soon. Still, with no new ambassador in sight, but with a steady cash flow on the payroll, I saw an opportunity to fly back to Ghana to visit my family, especially to see my new boy after almost a year of being in the United States. So in February of 2004, I booked a flight to travel down to see my family. My joy was over the moon as my eyes lit with anticipation. On the flight, I created, played and recreated various scenes of how I imagined the welcome reception would be back at home.

# Chapter 12

# Chapter 12

Touchdown Ghana! Seeing my wife and kids Gilbert and Cecelia at the airport with grins was all the warmth I had craved. The ride home to Dansoman was calm. My beautiful Sarah leaned against my chest as we shared an affectionate kiss, thereafter recounting all the memories created in my absence. She had remarkably held down the fort at home while working 12 hours a day as a banquet chef at the Golden Tulip Accra Hotel. About 3 hours into my arrival Sarah was phoned by a representative at the foreign affairs ministry to pick up her passport with her approved five-year A2 diplomatic visa. Two weeks before my arrival she had gone over to the ministry with my father-in-law to submit her passport to aid in the visa application and processing to have her join me in the United States. Things were looking up at this point.

The embrace of the warm heat, loud honks from road rage among drivers with a topping of loud conversations among neighbours from across the street, was all I had hoped a welcome back to Ghana atmosphere would be. I looked vacantly towards the gate from my little front porch as Sarah prepared to serve dinner. I figured it would be a good time to spill my random thoughts on her sojourn to the USA.
"Abakumah" I called after settling onto the nearest Kitchen stool. "You would have to come with me on my return to America."
She turned with her eyes squint, "This soon? I was considering coming on a visit after I wean Junior off breastfeeding and when he's independent enough to feed on his own. Which reminds me,

why were you unable to file for the kids?" That was a question I failed to answer at the moment. Cobbling up plans was more of my thing. Sarah liked to strategize on taking premeditated steps towards a goal. She fumed at my idea for her to "ditch" the kids to follow me to America.

"I'm not saying we should ditch the kids. They are mine as well. Look Abakumah, I have thought of ways we could both work together in America, and save enough to improve our living conditions. As it stands, my fate at the embassy is hanging in uncertainty yet coming back to Ghana to raise our children with meagre earnings would be unwise. Please come with me and together we could even end up going on early retirement." I managed to voice out without coming off as condescending. The final bit was to make her laugh yet Sarah stood firmly in the red zone. Was I being overly ambitious in my quest?

I strived for a better future for our children and together with Sarah. I believed we could reap more in the land of opportunities faster. I knew that leaving the kids, particularly Junior behind, would lay heavily on her thoughts. The first two, Cecelia and Gilbert were seven and four years old respectively and enrolled in an educational complex, Junior on the other hand was barely a year old and still attached to his mother's bosom. Previously elated by the earlier visa approval, the issue of suddenly moving without the kids quickly brought a dim in Sarah's mood.

We were scheduled to get on board a Ghana Airways Flight to the USA before it was banned by the US Department of Transportation (USDOT) from operating in or out of the United States. Well, according to a report by USA Today on 28 July 2004, with the bold headline, **"Ghana Airways banned in the United States."** The Flag carrier of Ghana had *ignored orders relating to the grounding of unsafe aircraft and that the airline had been operating on an out-of-date license. As a result, the airline was forced to cancel two weekly flights to Baltimore*

*—Washington International Airport and JFK International Airport.* The Spokesman of the USDOT added that the airline had utilized an aircraft which had been ordered by the Federal Aviation Administration to be grounded on the flight to New York City and Baltimore on 24th and 26th July 2004 respectively. Sadly the banning led to the sacking of the entire board of Ghana Airways and the Government taking full control of the airline *[BBC News, 13th August 2004]*. Besides the coat of Arms, I believed that Ghanaians wore the major Flag Airways as some sort of a badge of honour till our pride was completely wiped off. Moving forward, Sarah and I planned to make it early to the Kotoka International Airport, check-in and return home quickly to bid a proper farewell to our Cecelia and Gilbert, who had been sent off to school earlier. We pictured we had saved a lot more hours to hug them for the final time before departure. Oddly, the attendant at the counter informed us of the limited time we had between check-in and departure. What that implied was that we could not go back home to see our babies. And Sarah wept. My wife was in tears through the security checks, on the flight till we arrived in America. I was equally far from being "just fine" with what strangely occurred at the Airport. Still, I believed that God was up to something good hence the occurrence at the Airport. Back home, Sarah didn't have to answer to anyone except for the landlord. She lived comfortably with her children in her own home in her bed with room to toss and turn. My lady did not have to be a nuisance to anyone but upon arrival in the USA, that story was about to change. In our discussions back in Ghana regarding her trip to America, I hid crucial information regarding her accommodation. The Sarah I married would have vehemently refused to come with me if I had notified her of the arrangements made with a female work colleague to accommodate her in their home. She had always despised the thought or idea of becoming a case of

"inconvenience" to people. We drove straight from the airport to a friend's residence at Langley Park, Maryland which was about 25 minutes away from the Potomac residence. After a round of introduction, Sarah posed the dreaded question to me in a whisper, "Honey, this place is a two-bedroom house o. for the couple, the other for the kids, so where exactly would I be sleeping...with the kids?" "No dear, you see, things are quite expensive here in America and I'm currently the only one with an active job here. We aren't permitted to share our quarters at the residence with our spouses so, my friend has agreed to offer you the couch in the living room." "Huh!?" she yelled. I believe she instantly understood why I was yet to file for the kids. Where would they be crammed into their mother's bosom on the floor or a stranger's couch? The thought of her squeezing her curves into a tiny couch with her luggage pushed into the mini coat closet close to the exit hit me hard. Had I failed as a man? No, deep down I believed Sarah understood my reasons to some extent. to strive together in a foreign land to create a haven for our future and that of our kids. I departed the Potomac residence with a heavy heart.

Sarah recounts the many nights she cried on the velvet couch questioning why she had to subject herself to such living conditions away from her children. She recalls the suffocating times she had to gather her clothes, pomades and everything she'd need from the little coat closet in the living room to take into the shower with her. On weekends, she was mostly stationed in the kitchen because the offspring of her generous hosts occupied her sleeping space to enjoy some good hours of television. Before her hosts would depart for work she'd instruct Sarah on the meal preference for the day. The lady of the house would often ask Sarah before heading out to work, "Sis, what are we eating today?", "Sis can you make soup?" can you do that?

She had to put up with all that — As long as she occupied their couch rent-free, she had to pay for it somehow. It was her duty to ensure that everyone returned to a home-cooked meal. This was America after all!

**In July 2004**, the Embassy of Ghana geared up for the arrival of their newly appointed Ambassador under Former President Kuffour. The freshly appointed representative, succeeding Hon. Alan Kyeremateng was to assume duty as Ghana's Ambassador to the USA (with concurrent accreditation to Mexico, Guatemala, Belize, Haiti and the Bahamas) by the end of July that year. With over thirty years of experience in diplomatic practice, **Ambassador Fritz Kwabena Poku,** who additionally was a barrister at Law, was set to lead the embassy with his expertise garnered from years serving various international bodies including World Trade Organisation (WTO) in Geneva, Switzerland, International Atomic Energy Agency (IAEA) among others. While others made merry at the news, Frank and I prepared to exit the Residence because the Ambassador, was expected with his entourage including a Chef, a Butler and a Personal Aide. Our salaries had been cut off a month prior so at this point, we were disposable. It's always easy for one to escape the truth of reality in the comfort of a moment. Yet without a place of my own away from the cushioned life at the Potomac residence, I journeyed to join my wife as an extra occupant in my friend's living room. The Humiliation! As my wife would end most of her days cooking, cleaning and scrubbing for our hosts, she'd retire to the couch while I'd lie in the open space on the floor next to the couch. For a brief moment, I was under the impression that monetary issues from my childhood had tailed me in my new beginning. The complaints began rolling in, my wife had had enough. She had spent six months subjecting herself to stress and discomfort away from her children and had missed Junior's first birthday while being unproductive in America. She pulled me aside one weekend for a walk to address the issue at hand.

"I can't continue living here like this. I am technically working as a maid to these people because of their kind gesture." She proceeded, "Please get yourself an apartment so we can move in together or I'll hop on the next available flight to Ghana and will only return when you're settled."

She was right but I couldn't let her go. "You aren't going anywhere Abakumah, we'll find us a job and soon it'll all come together you'll see. We'll rent a one-bedroom apartment and move in together." I replied pulling her closer to my side. It was all the fire I needed to shift from the "has been" to the" will be."

After 3 weeks of unsuccessful attempts at securing proper work, I chanced upon an offer I believed could aid Sarah and me to secure an apartment. In a rickety windowless second-hand Hyundai accent car I had purchased, one evening we drove to a large warehouse in Silver Spring, Maryland and before I could provide an explanation on anything, Sarah began throwing her many questions from her curious mind. "Honey, what is this place? What are those guys busily gathering over there? Is this some kind of production house?"

I answered, "Dear, I'm sure you've noticed the people who come around throwing newspapers from block to block every morning?"

"Yes, I have."

"Good. This is the warehouse we'll be operating from. At 2 am every morning we'll come over to bag the newspapers before distribution."

"Ah! Joojo, so is this the job you proudly spoke about? How are we to go about the distribution? In this car which starts like an angry train?" she roared with laughter. "Well, if this would help us secure our apartment then I'm in."

Felt good to have her humour revived. It was a signal of approval for what needed to be done. With plastic sheets in place of glass, we drove through the cold to the warehouse every day at 2 am to collect our papers for distribution. There were no technicalities involved in sharing newspapers. It only required good arm strength to swing the papers as far as possible to the various demarcated doorsteps per list. There were a few unfortunate days where we had to park our shacky car to climb a flight of stairs into various apartment buildings to meet our target delivery of the day.

We were ingenious enough to overcome the limited supply of income to save a sufficient amount together to rent a one-bedroom apartment in White Oak, Maryland. Sarah's smile was ear to ear, inarguably her happiest day in America. After the deposit, the apartment managers needed to conduct some necessary checks before handing over the keys but Sarah insisted on moving in while the checks were ongoing. She could no longer wait to sleep in whichever position she desired without a cause to stay alert or worry about being uncovered or caught slipping in her sleep in any way. Sarah smiled more in an empty apartment than in the furnished one at Langley Park. She soundly slept on duvets on the floor and hopped up at dawn and had a definite spring in her step since we secured the job with the warehouse. Digging a little into our earnings, we purchased essential utensils to cook for ourselves as we continued to wander the streets of America without proper documentation though, still with a valid visa. What does the Psalmist say in Psalm 23:1? The Lord is my Shepherd, I lack nothing. Indeed, He provided bedding and helped furnish our apartment in the most unanticipated way. The affluent neighbourhoods with elaborate buildings of Silver Springs were occupied by rich inhabitants who often discarded their slightly used furniture at a

dump after less than 6 months of acquisition. We happened to have driven by one such dump one Friday night during one of our daily dawn work shifts. The presence of several U-Haul trucks dropping off this furniture one after the other without looking back was quite intriguing to us.
"Are they disposing of them?" She asked
"Yeah"
"But why would they do that when the furniture is in good condition?"
"Well, that's the rich folks of America for you.'

"We have to go shopping." And we did. Those trucks came by every Friday night to discard the home rejects, so, with proper timing together with the aid of a U-haul we rented. My wife and I scavenged through the affluent junk for all we could take home. Boy did we hit the jackpot! We got a couch, dining table, a television set, a coffee table, a mattress and a few more which were in the most perfect condition. By the break of morn, we had a fully furnished apartment. We proceeded to make plans for the weekend. Sit back on our new couch, enjoy some good homemade food and explore American channels on our new television. Once we grabbed the remote and switched on the TV, we realized that the lower half of the screen had completely blacked out.

Sarah said amid laughter, "Oh well, as long as we are seeing the faces of the people without their legs, we'll enjoy it." What a woman!

Before being discharged by the Embassy of Ghana, I had filed for all three of my children to join us in the United States. The Embassy was far advanced before I was relieved of duty. While on our wanderings between White Oak and Silver Springs I still wasn't quite settled on the fate of their visas. There was the constant drumming thought of how they were going to be allowed entry into the United States. Truth be told, Sarah and I had decided to settle in America which in our view was a hub of countless opportunities to work and earn twice more than we earned in Ghana per month. We were also of the belief that our kids would have access to quality education and a life we never had growing up in Ghana if only given the chance to join us. Isn't that all we strived for as parents…to seek out the best in everything for our kids and hopefully the next generation to come? That fire burns the brightest when you have tasted poverty in the most humiliating manner. For me, it was bothersome to not be in control or oversee the entire application process for my kids.

Then Jireh showed up again to provide most miraculously. Back home in Ghana, the children had received dates for their scheduled interview appointment at the US Embassy on 24 fourth circular Rd. in Accra. Mr. Vroom, My father-in-law, had offered to take the kids to have their interview on the due date. Restlessness got the best part of my day. The constant calls for updates and briefs on the appearance and composure of the kids pretty much summed up my activities. It was a gamble from that point. Just when I was about to kick the weight off, I received a call from a rather unfamiliar number. Strangely, it was the consular at the US Embassy in Ghana calling to make some enquiries.

"Is Mr. Otoo still working at the Embassy of Ghana?" asked the thin feminine voice on the other side of the line.
"Yes, he still works at the embassy," I answered without hesitation.
"Okay, we needed this confirmation to proceed with his children's visa."
"Oh Yes! He still works with us so kindly go ahead to assist him

with whatever needs to be done." I replied in a tone exuding confidence.

"Sure. Thank you." The line went dead.

Turned out, the consular, in her attempt to contact staff at the Embassy of Ghana, strangely ended up dialling my number. I panicked. I had just spewed a lie to a United States government official. What if she had already contacted someone else from the embassy regarding my real status and this was all a set-up? Had I jeopardized the chance of securing visas for my kids? My conscience ate me up. As I submerged deeper into my thoughts, I was startled by a phone call from my father-in-law. Recalling his exact words, he said, "Thank God, the children's visas have been granted." I sighed in relief. Then came the aha moment when I looked at my call log. The outcome would have been the contrary if the consular had directly called the embassy. Stunned, I stood with my eyes fixated on the sky as if to say, "I knew that was you, God. Thank you." Sarah was elated after I broke the news to her. She gave me the tightest hug and giggled in sheer delight. To celebrate, we took a quick drive in our rickety car to plan the next steps to take.

My very first credit card in the United States was issued around this period. I vividly remember having a credit of about $ 3,000. We already set plans in motion to purchase tickets for Sarah and the kids. We thought it wise not to leave the country together to go fetch the kids together. Fostering superstitious beliefs that 'something' from 'somewhere' could try to hinder all five of us from entering the United States if we both exited to Ghana to bring the kids. Guess I was still paranoid about the lie told to the consular and also harboured the fear of being stripped of the little progress we had both struggled to make financially in the United States. My wife continues to tease me to date about how I paced our apartment saying, *"Please we need not wait to work extra shifts for a month to get the kids. If we wait too long before these people overturn their decision."* Though they had obtained the visa, we were quite sceptical of what could be. Quickly, I dispatched my wife to Ghana to prepare the kids for departure while I stayed behind and continued to work the newspaper distribution shift. Sarah found it nearly impossible to cope without the children after being away from them for over a year. I had equally missed them as well.

Junior cried whenever Sarah stood as much as an inch away from him. Could you blame him? He didn't make her out at all. He had only spent seven months feeding from her breast at a time when his brain wasn't fully prepared to process memories. Cecilia and Gilbert, on the other hand, could not be separated from their mother. Like a protective mother duck with her ducklings, they followed wherever she led. The children were left under the care of Sarah's twin, Ruby Vroom, who Junior recognized as his mother. After two weeks of observing his older siblings run up to Sarah all the time calling her Mama, he finally warmed up to her. Packing a few of each of their clothes into a single suitcase after exhausting about 4 weeks in Ghana, they bade farewell to Ruby Vroom and Madam Hammond to begin a trip to a new beginning. On May 3rd 2005, my woman embarked on a journey to America with three little children, on board a KLM flight on transit at Schipol Airport Amsterdam and scheduled to arrive at Dulles International Airport on May 4th 2005, Junior's second birthday. Picture the chaos of travelling through the massive Schipol Airport with three minors who had tendencies to bolt at any given time. Should luck evade you, you might end up missing your flight for good. The struggles of travelling with kids, trying to keep an eye on their every move, yelling as a signal to keep them alert, and getting them to stay comported on and off flight could be quite tiring for even the strongest of women. It was all over her face as she emerged from the arrivals section, from the way she walked, you could tell that her limbs were drained of all energy from probably running around to keep those kids in check.

# Chapter 13

# Chapter 13

Drama, it seemed, was the biggest fan of my early life in America. After waiting close to an hour watching tons of people checking out to exit the airport to meet their families with hugs and cheers, My family was still nowhere in sight. Troubled, I walked to the counter to verify if all the passengers on board the KLM flight from Accra –Amsterdam had all checked out, and she said yes. My eyes widely circled, scanning through the entire section where I stood. Fortunately, I heard an announcement on the airport's intercom.

*"If Mr. Otoo is here, we would kindly like to see him at the Immigration."*

I did the exact opposite of what the announcer requested, I ran straight towards the exit for the parking lot where I stood again for over thirty minutes. "Not today" I muttered under my breath, "You won't get me today, it's not happening." An hour later I decided to walk inside to surrender to whatever reason I was needed at the immigration, perhaps, God may show us Mercy again. I got out of the car, walked to the arrival hall again and there was Sarah with our kids all teary-eyed. We shared minutes of big warm hugs till I quickly stepped back and told them to let exit the airport before they change their minds concerning whatever happened in there. We swaddled the kids into the back seat of the car and then Sarah proceeded to furnish me with details of what happened at the immigration. Far from a cause for alarm, it was for our good. As stated earlier, my wife and I had gained entry into the USA on an A2 diplomatic visa while our kids were placed on A3 domestic visas. This pointed to the fact that they were recognized as domestic workers, not diplomats. In summary, I was summoned by immigration to be given an official note to send over to the State Department for my kids to be upgraded to diplomatic visas. Back then, I believed that my visa would be revoked due to the termination of my appointment by the Embassy of Ghana. I had perceived that I was probably on the US immigration's most wanted list — ignorance! You can imagine my gratitude to God after Sarah ended her narration. A meeting with the immigration would have been needless because there were no records of me being an employee of the Embassy within the past year. We thought it best to let their generosity slide in order not to cause a stir of legal issues. At the end of the day I had my family together safely in one space — my circle was full.

Government Schools in America were tuition free. The State only required students to undergo medical screenings to be approved for enrollment. They also required proof of infant vaccination and birth certificates to ensure they were beyond the age of five and also to facilitate the admission process. Cecelia and Gilbert were approved by the state for enrolment at Bethesda Elementary while Junior stayed back at daycare. With the kids around, Sarah had to let go of the job at the newspaper warehouse to prepare them for school while I stayed in the rush to steady the in-flow of our daily bread. From the year she clocked an "employable" age till date, Sarah has always been on the go. Striding with a *can't stop won't stop* attitude wherever she was planted. So it came as no surprise when she got herself two jobs almost immediately. From 10 pm she worked as a janitor for the management offices of Marriot hotel in Maryland, and from 9 am to 2 pm as a cook at Hebrew Home of Greater Washington, a nursing home in North Bethesda, Maryland.

As days went by, I gained employment as a cook at **Maple wood Park Place**, a retirement community in Bethesda, Maryland. I was already late to my newspaper job one morning when I came across a gentleman standing next to the building I had exited. At a glance, I noticed he wore a chef's jacket which instantly piqued my interest. In a quick conversation, he pointed to the retirement home as his place of work and drew my attention to the open call for cooks at the restaurant in the care home. "I'm grateful brother, how do I apply?" I proceeded to enquire. The gentleman was patient enough to direct me to the various online portals through which I could apply for the job. In about a week I had earned a cooking spot at the kitchens of Maple wood Park Place after thinly considering my social security number and visa as my only work details. The HR manager took a final look at my credentials to only inform me of how the management thought I was over qualified for a 'mere' position as a cook. I said with a sigh "sir, At this point just let me work. After a while, if you still deem me overqualified for the position of a cook and there's any open vacancy, you could consider me for that." Truth was, I no longer had the joy of setting out at 2 am to hand out newspapers in the cold for a scanty wage. So Sarah would get the kids to school after I got them ready before gearing up for my 9-to-5 job, journey on to Hebrew Home for her morning shift to return in time to pick them up by 4 pm. This was the daily routine for members of the Otoo home.

Fall of 2005, we caught on with our ridiculous monthly expenditure. Junior's daycare drained $250.00 from our coffers weekly. I know, it was ridiculous. Wages from Sarah's morning shift covered the daycare charges while that from her night shifts were used additionally with mine to cover our monthly $800.00 rent, bills, food, emergencies and whatever 'pop-ups' we might have the urgency to pay for. I contended with having my son enrolled in daycare and managed to convince Sarah to stay home to cater for her son. It was needless to be left in the red after committing an entire earning from the care home to daycare fees — she was better off taking care of her son by herself. I'd take over catering for the kids after my nine-hour work shift to allow Sarah to ease into her night janitorial duties at the Marriott hotel where she bi-weekly earned $1,100.

Maple Wood Park Place was the Challenge I longed for, dissimilar to my early years of cooking at the embassy of Ghana, yet availed the opportunities to create, learn and unlearn new ways of cooking for people with specific nutrition demands and needs. My new job afford me a sense of importance and a chance to gain work experience in an area that sort of worked in-hand with the medical personnel in creating meals tailored to our client's needs. I was finally back to doing what I loved after taking a much-needed detour in my quest to earn a living to survive in America. I wore my Chef's jacket with pride. After about a year at Maplewood, there came a sudden urge to move. The desire to begin afresh in a new space. I'm guessing it was simply because, like with the uncertainties that came with migrating with family, there was always the assumption that I could do better or earn more elsewhere to give my family some comfort. After all, they relocated here at my insistence. I continued in my application for a new job while at the post at Maplewood Park Place. I received some favourable news about a month later, after qualifying for an interview with **the Hilton Alexandria Mark Centre**. So after months of serving as a cook at Maple wood, I folded things up to begin as a Supervisor at the Hilton Alexandria in September 2006, where I continued to work with my Social Security number and visa. Working at the Hilton Alexandria was a lot like working back in Ghana. My experiences garnered from working with the Golden Tulip and

La Palm Royal Beach Hotel came very much in handy at my new job. As a supervisor — again for a section of the kitchen, I saw to the preparation of healthy and safe meals while following all laid down health and hygiene regulations. Also coaching and directing all kitchen staff in ensuring that the kitchen service areas are kept tidy at all times. The Hilton Alexandria reminded me more of my days at the La Palm than the Golden Tulip. Mainly because of how I worked closely with kitchen staff in catering for the many dignitaries who thronged the high-rise space for both work and pleasure. To paint a little picture of my new working space, The Hilton Alexandria stood five miles from downtown Washington within the west end of historic Alexandria. Its location offered a peaceful lakeside setting providing stylish rooms with breathtaking views of DC. The hotel boasted modern-styled rooms numbering about 430, palatial indoor spaces plus an outdoor and gazebo for all events. My description isn't doing the needed justice to this edifice, you'd have to be there to soak it all in for yourself.

Archbishop Desmond Mpilo Tutu, the late South African theologian and Nobel Prize winner, was revered for his role as a leading unifying personality and a catalyst for change in the campaign during the period of apartheid, which upheld segregationist policies against non-white citizens in South Africa, which eventually came to an end in the early 90s. Under the invitation of Former U.S President, George W. Bush, the late Desmond Tutu visited the United States where he lodged at the Hilton Alexandria. As the only African Chef at the hotel, I was specially assigned to cater to his daily sustenance. Look, I cannot begin to express the blend of emotions which flooded my mind as I sat next to this larger-than-life personality, taking note of his nutritional preferences and possible allergies…unbelievable! Occasionally rubbing my eyes in disbelief, I tried to rein in my dispersed thoughts to maintain a good composure. God ordered my steps and had me at the right place at the right time. Our relationship sometimes went a little beyond a client and a chef. We shared a laugh or two and spoke briefly about our mother continent — Africa. Moments so priceless, I kept them under lock and key in the safety of my memories.

After about a year of serving as a Supervisor, I got promoted to a banquet chef early in January 2008 which came with additional benefits and a slight bump in salary. On the downside, this advancement in my career came at a time my visa had expired. Of course, I stayed quiet about it till the management brought in a new HR manager who as part of her duties, began examining all personnel files and documents. Upon noticing that my visa had expired, she called me privately into her office for questioning. Though I had been exposed, I replied as though there were proceedings in the pipeline to resolve the visa issue. The HR manager handled the issue with leniency and relieved me of my duties for some time to resolve the issue with immigration and return with a new visa. "Of course" I responded in a tone marred with shame. I deliberately overstayed the given period because I knew there was absolutely no way I was going to acquire another visa. In line with that, I dismissed myself and continued to stay at home with my children. In all the happenings with my job, I however continued to apply for jobs with institutions outside of Hilton Alexandria with no luck. I didn't want anyone blowing my cover on the expired visa. My wife's visa was close to expiration and so were my kids. Then I became of the conviction that the Otoos were finally on the verge of deportation. I had come to a point where everything pointed to returning to Ghana. It was deeply troubling. We had no business with The Embassy of Ghana so it would certainly be beyond unreasonable to call on them for a favour. I was even sure it could trigger alarms for deportation. Sarah— again brought my mind to order with her timely words of wisdom.

*"Dear, I believe that God has equipped us with impeccable skills with which could make a living. You came into this country on the ticket of the Embassy of Ghana as a chef but unfortunately, that was short-lived. I think we should kick start the catering business here in America as we did together in Ghana to see how far we could go. You never know what the good Lord has aligned in our favour."* As with a melody she caught my attention. Sarah was right, it would be best to get something started on the low with what I had saved from my previous jobs to at least 'keep me occupied for a while, I thought. We started by offering to cater for various events and occasions in our church including the annual youth camp which hosted a total of 700 people, the Royal Ladies Conference which saw a gathering of about 800 ladies and the annual convention of saints where a total of 300 men of God from various continents converge under an atmosphere to worship.

In America, my family and I worshipped at the Laurel, Maryland branch of the Royalhouse Chapel, Ahenfie under the stewardship of Apostle Emmanuel Agormerdah whom I had met in Ghana before being poached from La Palm by the Embassy of Ghana. In addition to being a senior pastor of the Royalhouse Chapel International (RHCI) churches in North America including Mexico, the United States and Canada for the past 19 years. He is a full-time preacher, Revivalist, speaker and counsellor. I encountered Apostle Agormerdah in the year 2000 when I served some VVIPs at the Residence of the Apostle General. There was no room to make conversation or to get acquainted with each other. He happened to have been dispatched by the Apostle General to steward the RHCI branches in the United States the same year I arrived in the States. I happened to have catered for his wedding that same year. At the formative stages of the RHCI Maryland, my family and I were among the first few members of the congregation who became committed to the vision of the service. Since then, the rest is history. he has turned out to be the man, who has shown interest in journeying with me towards the completion of my purpose, praying with me and guiding me towards making crucial decisions in my career and life as a whole on a personal level — My spiritual father. Through catering for the church, our name spread throughout the Ghanaian community in Washington. Whenever anyone needed catering of any kind, Apostle Agormerdah would entreat them to call on us. Of course, it wasn't after they'd had a taste of the authentic flavouring of our well-prepared dishes. Every order was cooked and packaged from the tiny kitchen which opened to our living room in our one-bedroom apartment in White Oak. In place of an air freshener, the atmosphere in our room reeked of an unbalanced mixture of varieties of aromas. We had people calling in on weekends to place personal orders for meals on and off our recited menu. They would drop by the apartment or opt for a courier to pick them up on their behalf. Cecelia and Gilbert were our little packaging personnel on extremely busy days while Junior was kept in a corner either playing or causing mayhem. These scenes played out in our home almost every week till all our visas expired; my wife's, my kids and mine. We resided illegally in America, catering for our church while keeping a low profile. It would be a shame to sully our travel history if we were caught by US immigration. Something as basic as the siren of an ambulance triggered some level of paranoia as if our cover had been blown somehow. Certainly, a burdensome way to walk the streets of America. With no hope of revival in sight, we submitted to the status of illegal migrant whose contingency plan was probably to forge marriages with a citizen who would then adopt our kids to earn residency status. It was something Sarah and I had painfully brought ourselves to discuss. ..It would be a betrayal to our family by travestying our marriage in our quest for legal immigration status.

At some point during all the wine and dine at the RHCI, I stood shoulder-to-shoulder with Apostle Agormerdah sometime in March 2008, as he gracefully introduced me one after the other to curious guests who sought to pay their compliments to the chef. Throughout the entire evening, I recorded some people, mostly women, probing my ingredient selection and the secret behind the natural flavouring in some meals. Among them was a middle-aged Nigerian woman who stood behind the gathering, waiting on her turn to either pay compliments or make an enquiry.

"*Ah*! Chef, you've left quite an impression on my taste buds with your sumptuous meals." she began.
"I appreciate the compliment, madam," I answered in eagerness to hear what her question for me would be.
"Nah! Don't mention. It's almost like there's a story behind the distinct flavours of your well-curated meals. You have all the guests talking!"
I replied with a short laugh, "I try my best madam."
"Oh stop being modest. Anyway, I would like to introduce you to somebody."
"Of course, please lead the way."
"Oh no, he's not here. It's my uncle. He is the newly appointed Nigerian Ambassador to the USA. We have been on a hunt for a cook to hire officially to serve him and the embassy as the in-house chef."
She caught the rest of my attention from this point. "Oh really?" I asked in astonishment.
"Yes! Let me have your phone number. I'll arrange to have you

come over to the embassy to officially introduce you to him." She turned to walk away after exchanging contact numbers. Just as I was about to look away she quickly turned, "one more thing Chef, there wouldn't be a need for a cooking demonstration or a probationary period. Your meals tonight have sealed the deal. See you tomorrow."
I stood with my mouth agape for over a minute. Watching her smoothly exit like she just did not drop a bomb on me...the good kind.

**BG. CHRISTOPHER OLUWOLE ROTIMI (Rtd.)**, former Nigerian Ambassador to the USA was a retired Nigerian Army Brigadier General, diplomat and politician who was preceded by George Obiozor, also a diplomat and a Nigeria professor. From April 1971 to July 1972, Oluwole Rotimi happened to be the Governor of the Western State while Nigeria was under military rule. He was almost instantly enamoured by my personality which he described as "courteous." He asked jokingly after a full 15-minute food and culture-centred conversation, "Can you start today?" he had offered me the job immediately. I answered, "Well, I could even begin in the next second if you'd permit Me." there was no time to take chances. I intended to step on the accelerator on this opportunity before they had room to entertain doubts.

Rev. Sam Korankye Ankrah, the Apostle General, had travelled to the United States for the 2008 edition of the annual Convention of Saints Conference. It was within the same period the Nigerian embassy had requested that I brought in my passport together with my family's to the residence for them to be sent to the State Department for Visa renewal. Remember the State Department? The same office whose 'summon' I had evaded over the years. I stood petrified for a moment by the table of the embassy official to whom we handed our passports. I reasoned that the State Department upon noticing the expired visas could hand us over the US Immigration for deportation. I grew more sceptical by the day. every minute of the five working days we had to wait for a response from the State Department was pure torture. At the end of the day's service, he called for a seed of $500.00 and I recall having almost $1,000.00 left in my account. Quickly, I stepped outside to the ATM to withdraw the requested seed, placed it in a sealed envelope and dropped it at the altar. He said to me, "Before the end of the convention, whatever has been a stumbling block to your heart desires will be levelled out of the way and you shall surely receive your innermost desire." To the glory of God, by the time the convention came to end, no damning questions were asked by the State's Department or the Embassy pertaining to our visas and all five of us were handed our passports with work permits. Look at God! Cecelia and her little brothers were yet to attain working age yet, they were cleared for a work permit. Just at the time we had expired visas, Jehovah Jireh showed up with diplomatic visas with extra work permits for us to behold his glory in full force. We were all given A2 diplomatic visas under the seal of the Nigerian embassy.

It had earmarked the beginning of a new era, hired under a new leader and overseen by a different umbrella of culture. The sub-Saharan African countries of Ghana and Nigeria possess some striking similarities in culture yet slightly varying culinary methods. The choice of cooking herbs and ingredients, and the practical step-by-step procedure in cooking could probably create quite an argument among native culinary experts from both countries if placed together in a shared kitchen. When it came to foods enjoyed by both countries, one could not go without mentioning the obvious similarities like black-eyed pea fritters popularly known as k*oose* in Ghana and as a*kara* in Nigeria, j*ba* which is gari soaked with hot water and moulded into balls and enjoyed with stew or soup in some cases and then there is the famous Jollof rice through which a famous war erupted per which I'll reserve my controversial comments for now.

With the knowledge I had garnered over the years from studying and serving distinct foreign nationals, it was no trouble fitting into my new space. Knowing which meal to serve at what time and which native flavouring to use came in handy. At the embassy, Ambassador Rotimi became completely fond of my *Moi-Moi, Egusi* soup and j*ba* though I served an assortment of delicacies from across continents. We seldom had left over at the residence after meals and that alone was a pat on the back. Whenever visiting dignitaries came knocking, Ambassador Rotimi overstated my culinary skills in a manner which kept our guests looking forward to the menu of the day. Rotimi was quite accommodating for an army officer who had lived through a chaotic military regime. I commuted every day for work, unlike at the Embassy of Ghana where I had more of a live-in situation. At 6 am every weekday I would drive my rickety car to work or hop on the bus to make it in time to set up and serve breakfast and then retire for the day when the last working staff exits the premises. Sarah kept the family train going. Getting the kids ready for school, keeping them in check while adjusting the remainder of the time to making it for work and tending to herself each day. With support from my superwoman, we continued to keep our little catering business afloat on weekends even on occasional emergency absences. All members of the Otoo home were filled with optimism over the subsequent 365 days until Ambassador Rotimi was re-called by the former president of Nigeria, Alhaji Umaru Musa Yar'Adua after allegations of gross insubordination. I was taken aback by it. According to a publication by *Emeka Nwosu* sighted on allafrica.com retrieved in 2009, *Ambassador Rotimi was reported to have been running a disagreement with former Nigerian foreign affairs minister, Chief Oju Maduekwe over issues bordering policy, protocol, hierarchy and management of Nigeria's mission in Washington.* Their altercations reportedly resulted in an exchange of a series of correspondences which saw a pinnacle of a letter written by Ambassador Rotimi allegedly referring *to Maduekwe as a tribalist among other unprintable remarks.* The embassy staff was thrown into a state of bewilderment. each one consumed in never-ending photographic thoughts of what would eventually become of their fate at the embassy.

Early September 2008, less than a year of working with the Nigerian embassy, a farewell party was organized for Rotimi in line with his dismissal from the embassy. I recall preparing a variety of dishes, each meal honouring various countries and cultural backgrounds of invited dignitaries. I recall receiving members of the embassies of Togo, Ivory Coast, Senegal, Burkina Faso and of course Ghana in the USA. Ghana's Ambassador at the time, **Kwame Bawuah Edusei**, A Ghanaian physician, entrepreneur and diplomat who had previously served as Ghana's Ambassador to Switzerland from 2004-2006, attended the function in the company of Ambassador Martha Akyaa Pobee, the then Head of Chancery for the Embassy of Ghana. After hours exhausted from feasting with the departing ambassador, Mrs Pobee approached me simply from the point of being a Ghanaian in a Nigerian setting. Everyone at the soiree talked about the Ghanaian chef at the Embassy of Nigeria who prepared and served the sumptuous cultural variety of meals they had enjoyed. Ambassador Rotimi had indicated with pride that the chef of the night was Ghanaian, so she wondered what I was doing in that space.

"Are you Ghanaian?"
"Yes" I answered.
"I see. What is your name?"
"Francis Otoo"
"Your name rings a bell, Francis Otoo...Francis Otoo." She sung repeatedly, looking upwards as if to fish out a memory from the sky.
She continued, "Do you know Miss Laine?"
I stared in her eyes in confusion.
"Do you recall being at Accra Polytechnic at any point in time?"
I said with excitement, "oh yes, yes! That's my former school Oh! Miss Laine formerly headed the catering department"
"Ah good. Do you recall being at my wedding in 1994?"
I paused in a moment of reflection as she proceeded to jog my memory with a back story of her wedding
"Oh yes yes, I now remember you. I was still a schoolboy at the time. Your wedding was at the Ford Foundation on the University of Ghana campus"
"Yes you were. I never forget a face."
"Of course, you don't, this moment attests to that," I replied with a nervous laugh.
She had taken me by surprise because we barely interacted at her wedding. I merely waited at the occasion so it was quite astonishing that she made me out after so many years had gone by. Perhaps, like she tells me today, my head had truly stuck out on my tall body over everyone else's at the wedding.
"Francis what are you doing pouring out all your talent in serving our Nigerian counterparts *ehr*? When those of us at the embassy of your motherland are currently in need of an official cook?"
I sighed in response, "Madam, *woakofa asjm aba*, you have

brought up a dire issue." I further elaborated on how I had been discharged by the embassy of Ghana due to politically motivated reasons which in a way, was about to repeat itself at the Nigerian Embassy, because at the embassy of Ghana, Hon. Alan Kyeremanteng was re-called back home to occupy a new Ministerial position which had me and a few others kicked out. And now, Ambassador Rotimi was at the exit to pave way for Tunde Adeniran who I had been informed was coming with his batch of aides and cooks. "Oh but that's not how it's supposed to be," She retorted. "Here's my card, please make time to see me at the office tomorrow. I'll be expecting you. As the Head of Chancery, she had the responsibility to organize official events which included hiring of caterers. So, with the way I performed with professionalism, she expounded on her observation that, she could tell that I enjoyed what I did with passion. Much later that night, Ambassador Pobee combed through her photo albums and there indeed I was. In the background with my busy body waiting tables and that was how it all connected.

With the Embassy of Ghana on the hunt for a cook and Oluwole Rotimi en route to Nigeria in the first trimester of the coming year. I, too, was in the midst of a transition. Looking out for a new job and clinging on to hope that some good news may rear its neck out soon. In a span of a short time, I had given myself to working with the Nigerians with a passion that, I found it draining when Rotimi's tenure came to an abrupt end. I had motives to stay longer than necessary because I was reluctant to let go of this job. Perhaps, it was with hopes that I may find favour in the sight of the arriving Ambassador, Tunde Adeniran, though it had been made clear to me on two separate occasions that I could no longer serve as a cook for either him or the embassy. Here's a little twist to the story, the embassy of Nigeria though had no use for me as a cook, was unwilling to cross me permanently out of their official employees' folder. Instead, I was offered the position to serve as a part-time security man at the embassy. The underlying reasons, which I believed fueled the retaining offer, were my work ethic and preceding humility.

After thorough discussions with my wife, we came to a common agreement, which was to accept the embassy s offer to serve as a security man on part-time basis, solely in gratitude for securing and renewing our work permits and visas respectively. Sarah still held her faith that the same God who always worked things out in the nick of time would surely make another way for us. However, I followed up with Mrs Pobee on her open invitation to see her at the Embassy of Ghana to be introduced to the Ambassador. All the Ambassador could say regarding my employment situation was, "well, there's nothing specifically I could do about this but let's see how things will go from here." it was followed by an awkward back and forth circling the topic of my possible come back to the embassy. To keep the peace, I quietly coiled into my role, serving as a Security officer.

On the other hand, I continued to peek into the job market to see what was available for grabs. At least I had a renewed visa in addition to a work permit which made me confident with my search. Fortunately, I saw an open vacancy published by Maple Wood Park, my former place of work, seeking a kitchen supervisor. I applied and was assigned the role in a week. It took a great deal to properly manage my schedule to work both jobs because I wasn't prepared to let one go... I need the money for my family after all. My life activities have been back to back, without enough time for a breather. Surviving in America is not for the weak. Mrs Pobee, however, was relentless in her quest to get me back on the embassy of Ghana's staff list. It looked as though it was a 'tug-of-war between Mrs Pobee and the fate of my career with me as the flag or tied handkerchief in the middle of the endless rope of uncertainty. She knew what I carried and believed in me, probably more than I did in myself, hence the urgency to secure a 'rightful' position at the embassy. Ambassador Pobee, I believe, had pure intentions. As a Ghanaian, she strongly felt the need to promote my welfare. With the Nigerian Ambassador about to leave, there was no guarantee that I would be retained even on the security job. She thought for a talent such as mine, it would do the Ghanaian mission a lot of Good to put me on as a resident chef, if I may put it that way. All my life, I had barely come across people, who would go out of their way to play pivotal roles in aid of materializing the dreams or purpose of another individual, let alone a stranger.

# Chapter 14

# Chapter 14

Former President George Bush together with his spouse Mrs Laura Bush were pleased to welcome H.E John Agyekum Kuffour, former president of the Republic of Ghana with his wife Mrs Theresa Kuffour to the white house for a final visit as first citizens of Ghana. The Kuffours were received with equal generosity and hospitality rendered to the former president and Mrs Bush on their earlier visit to the West African country in February 2008.

In line with their visit, the two outgoing presidents were to discuss Ghana's effort to promote peace, democratic values and stability in Africa in addition to issues on combating malaria and other tropical diseases.

A state dinner was held in honour of H.E John Agyekum Kuffour and Mrs Theresa Kuffour at the State dining room at the white house in the presence of some dignitaries including Archbishop Nicholas Duncan Williams, founder of Christian Action Faith Chapel. The Honorable Rosa Whitaker, President and CEO, The Whitaker Group and spouse of Archbishop Nicholas Duncan Williams, Mr. Richard T O'Brien, President and CEO of the Newmont Mining. The children of H.E John and Mrs Theresa Kuffour namely Ms Helen Saah Kuffour, Mr. John Addo Kuffour, and Ms Nana Ama Kuffour among top management officials of the Millennium Challenge Corporations among a tall list of other dignitaries from across the globe.

The embassy of Ghana was in search of a chef who could accompany H.E John Agyekum Kuffour throughout his entire week stay in the United States. They required a Chef who was familiar with the terrain, equipped with all-round culinary skills and capable of privately catering for him and his entourage. Ambassador Martha Pobee — again proposed that she knew of a Chef whose skills and capabilities fit the requirement. Still, keen on securing my employment with the embassy, she proceeded to sing my praises and presented the Ambassador and his administrators with reasons she thought I deserved the spot. At some point in the discussion, Ambassador Pobee proceeded to give a brief back story. *"He catered for my wedding years ago and currently works at the Embassy of Nigeria in Washington. Can we put him on so he could travel with the President?"* She continued, *"I trust that he would be more than capable of executing all tasks among other duties that would be required of him."* She was yet to be informed that I had already accepted the offer to work as a security with the Nigerians. Soon after all documentation was done, Ambassador Pobee called in with the good news on behalf of Ambassador Edusei and the administration. It seemed so surreal! I would be attending to H.E John Agyekum Kuffour in America. I simply couldn't wait to share the news with Sarah, I knew she would scream and dance in excitement. Though it was only for a week, it felt as though it were for a lifetime. With my luggage ready after getting off my shift with the Embassy of Nigeria, I proceeded to Maple Wood Park Place for my night shift and also to speak with the manager to grant me a leave of absence for 8 days. After arriving at a common agreement to have me work some extra hours on my return, the request was approved.

I travelled to West Virginia with the former President and his entourage to The Greenbrier Hotel. It was a luxury 5 star hotel located somewhere in the Allegheny Mountains near White Sulphur Springs in greenbrier county. The luxury mountain resort had a spa, chains or retail shops, tennis, golf and other courts for various sporting activities. In my candid opinion, The Greenbrier was a complete paradise— a sweet escape from the reality I was used to. The spectacular landscape and manicured garden in view as you drive through the fine establishments, is more than capable of sweeping one off his feet. With a scenery almost therapeutic, it's safe to say that it is without a doubt a holiday haven. I briefly wandered into a day dream of how it would be to actually work in the kitchens of this establishment, which slowly transformed into motion pictures of Sarah and I having a good time at The Greenbrier, away from our daily hustles. It had rooms numbering over 700 and over 30 suites sitting on 11,000 acres of land and built over a ton of rich history. The Greenbrier site was said to be a bunker during the cold war. Let me furnish you with some extra detail, the bunker, was said to contain a number of dormitories, a power plant, clinic and even a cafeteria— I could say that added hugely to its allure. We checked into the presidential suite which, if my memory serves me right, had about 7 bedrooms which occupied two floors. The suite could be accessed by a private foyer. It had a library, a large living room with a dining area fit for royalty. I slept in a cottage attaché the suite which had its own dining area and kitchen. H.E John Agyekum Kuffour together with his crew would come in to eat at the cottage where I stayed and prepared all their meals.

I cooked and was accorded a rare opportunity to share quite personal moments with him. I was a living a page out of my wild imagination. There I was, chatting, sharing jokes and standing side by side this larger than life personality discussing the most random subjects. H.E John Agyekum Kuffour and his crew enjoyed my *Fufu* with Goat Light soup and *Omotuo*, with groundnut soup. Hear this, the authentic Ghanaian knows not to compromise with the originality of both pounded cassava and plantain fufu or its mixed fufu powder driven in a saucepan with the *bankuta* to create a starchy form. The starchy dish should always possess the perfect blend and taste of cassava, plantain or cocoyam, in order to sit well with its accompanied soup, preferably chicken, goat or beef light soup. *Omotuo* on the other hand is simply rice balls, made from boiled broken rice shaped into sizeable balls which is often paired with groundnut soup and a sea of protein with just right amount of ginger among other African herbs and spices. However, it's always important to inspect the quality of groundnut paste purchased before proceeding to make this meal. It would be humiliating to have your guests take turns to the bathroom to ease themselves of the meal you gracefully spent hours preparing.

Like former President Bill Clinton, H.E John Agyekum Kuffour enjoyed my boiled yam with *kontomire* stew. At that point, I was tempted to believe that my kontomire stew was without a doubt, my signature dish. Oh the compliments! There were almost no left over after serving this meal. The former President had warmed up to me to the extent that, he'd invite me out to jog together with him and some members of his crew. Unbelievable! It was beyond my wildest dream yet, there I was in my sweatpants and shirt, on a casual run with the gentle giant, H.E J.A Kuffour. God really does show out when He shows up for his people.

We left for D.C after exhausting a week at the Greenbrier. The former President, after bidding his farewells, prepared to return to Ghana with his entourage in time for the 2008 presidential elections. On the other hand, I resumed working my shifts at Maple wood Park Place, and also tending to the Catering business I operated from home together with my wife. Perhaps it was about time we legitimized the business, I thought. I dreamt it, desired it yet, I could not follow it up with visiting the right offices or institutions to make the necessary enquiries. Fear still had it fangs in my neck because I was of the conviction that, if the authorities found out that we operated a food business from home as immigrants, it could somehow result in the cancellation of our visas. The enemy, being fully aware of the victories on the other side of faith, perseverance and determination, crippled and clouded my mind with "what ifs." The poison held me back from taking the much required step of faith till after nearly 2 years from the time at the Greenbrier. My own way of thinking had in a way, become the greatest enemy to my progress.

Moving on, the Embassy of Ghana reiterated their appreciation for executing the task of catering for the former president to perfection. 'Let's stay in touch,' they said. My overactive mind presumed it was a mere formality to get me out of the way. It was not tough cajoling myself into believing that, it was probably the end of the road and whatever hopes I had embraced towards working again with the embassy.

Powers changed after the December 2008 presidential elections. It had shifted from the **New Patriotic Party (NPP)** to the **National Democratic Congress (NDC),** where H.E John Agyekum Kuffour handed over to the late John Evans Atta Mills who became the 3$^{rd}$ President of the 4$^{th}$ Republic of Ghana on 7$^{th}$ January 2009. Ambassador Edusei stepped down from his office at the embassy to pave way for Ghana's next representative to the United States. However, the embassy was for some months without an ambassador till October 2009. In those periods of waiting and uncertainty, Ambassador Pobee however, kept in consistent touch with me. I took her remembrance of me as a reminder to keep my hopes of ever returning to the embassy, alive.

The late former President, John Evans Atta Mills, appointed **Daniel Ohene Agyekum**, A career diplomatic and a politician who had previously as the Ashanti Regional Chairman of the

National Democratic Congress (NDC) from 2005-2008. He also briefly served as the Minister of State in charge of Chieftaincy and state protocol under the late Jerry John Rawlings administration from 2000-2001, when his party lost power the Kuffour led NPP administration. Ambassador Pobee did not hesitate in engaging Ambassador Ohene Agyekum on my career status. The minute he assumed his role at the embassy, she went on about how she knew of a chef who served at her wedding, catered for the former Nigerian Ambassador and how she thought I was the best fit for the position of an official chef at the embassy. She argued that because the embassy organized many activities which were often catered for by the ambassador's chef, he mostly was unable to do all the cooking, serving, and every other thing by his lonesome. So, it made a lot of sense to make that argument to officially bring me back on and retain me on contract basis.

"Not to be dramatic sir but there is something about the way he put his dishes together. Always well balanced and with a unique taste. His is something you do not regularly come across." She interpreted.

Ambassador Ohene Agyekum begun, "I do agree with the fact that, it would be necessary for the embassy to have an official chef who would see to the welfare of our guests, especially at functions."

"Exactly my point sir."

"Well, I do trust your judgment, and if you say he is as good as he is then I will make that he is settled... how soon can this arrangement begin Martha?"

"Leave that to me sir. I'll have the paperwork set up immediately for your approval, thank you."

True to her words, Ambassador Martha Pobee proceeded to set things in motion. Look at God! And it was all without my knowledge. In a few days, I was invited to the Embassy of Ghana to pen my signature on a contract, which would make me the official chef of the embassy on a more permanent basis. It implied that, irrespective of the political party in power or whoever assumed the ambassadorial office, my post remained untouched — the agreement vividly established that. There was, however, some flexibility in working hours because I only had to work actively when there were functions and when dignified guests paid courtesy calls on the ambassador. Being the head of Chancery, Ambassador Pobee was no stranger to the regulations of the Foreign Service and rules governing the United States. She tried to ensure that everything fell in line with both Ghanaian and American rules so that I could operate without any anxiety. The only thing she couldn't argue for was a monthly salary. Though I was in the books as an official staff of the embassy, I wasn't on a monthly payroll because I only worked part-time and paid for my services rendered at Embassy functions.

Now that I had been gainfully employed by the embassy, I knew that if I served well, this contract could see me through to my official retirement. Troubles with our visas had been left in the past together with all other career uncertainties. This was a new beginning. I, however, continued to serve at the Maplewood Park Place while working at the Embassy. It was all about time balance. Yet, it became somehow of a struggle to keep my career and personal life in complete state of equilibrium. This multi-hyphen life did not afford me ample time to fully show up for my children, both at home and at school functions, which obviously, were perfect avenues to solidify the natural bond we shared. My wife talks about a time she squeezed her equally busy schedule to drive Gilbert and Francis to a basketball. I say this as a proud father that, both my sons are equally gifted in that sports field. Gilbert plays with the Men's basketball team at Trinity College while Francis plays for his team at the University of Maryland. Sarah recalls being half asleep as she drove the boys for their scheduled game. The moment Sarah pulled up at the parking lot, the boys rushed out of the car and walked hastily towards the entrance. My wife, sticking her neck out the window, yelled after them, "I'm right behind you guys...give me a moment to stretch my legs." In unison they replied, "Okay mum." She checked with the time and it about 45 minutes to the start of the game. She thought she could recline the seat for a 30 minute nap, touch up her makeup, and brush her hair with the remainder of the minutes to cheer the boys on. About 2 and half hours later, startled by a knock on the window, Sarah opened her eyes to see her two sweaty boys peeping through the glass.

"*Yei*," she exclaimed, "what's going on? Is it over already? How did you do?"

"Yeah mum, I made 15 points" Said Gilbert.

"Oh that's wonderful son. I should have been in there to watch you play but you know your mum, I'm still quite exhausted from my previous shifts."

"It's okay mum, I understand."

She didn't fully trust that they understood but she hoped they did. She drove in silence as the guilt she felt, weighed heavily on her shoulders. Sometimes she would plead with me to cancel out a work schedule or an appointment to show up for the boys, to which I followed through sometimes. The more time I spent out there committing to the various work schedules, the more I felt a little distant from my kids. Yet I knew one thing for sure, it was not to become my father. with this I make a daily conscious effort to be present and to share in their moments as often as possible, but naturally, the kids gravitated more towards their mother. I wonder how she does it, Sarah, how she managed to keep the entire house in one piece while juggling her multiple jobs and business. There is something peculiar about the mind of a woman

I couldn't quite comprehend. I'm tempted to believe that it is, perhaps made up of several mini compartments which are responsible for processing individual occurrences in specific areas of their lives. I also picture a wire chain connecting all these compartments together to somehow function in harmony. How they manage to get everything done is beyond me.

My wife, who from over the years had been tagged as a "madam busy body" by acquaintances obviously due to her frequent back and forth from her various shifts and swift moves as she dashed in one direction or the other grocery shopping, attending PTA function, and meeting prospective clients to seal new catering contracts and still make it home in time without burning out. When often asked to slow down by her peers, she would say, "This is America, You have to be busy or *kɛm bɜ de wo,* you'll go hungry." To this day, Sarah continues to embody the spirit of a hustler.

# Chapter 15

# Chapter 15

**His Excellency, the late President John Evans Fiifi Atta Mills,** visited the United States for the first time as President in September of 2009. He was arranged to meet and interact with the Ghanaian community in a town hall meeting at the auditorium of the Embassy of Ghana in Washington D.C. as stated earlier as part of her duties, Ambassador Pobee was tasked to organize the town hall meeting to introduce the President to the Ghanaian community in the United States. She, along with her team decided to make provisions for food and refreshment for all attendees. The idea to organize such meeting was quite the risk because. One could not predict whether the 100s of invitations sent out would be honored. Also, they were quite unsure of the President's schedule and at what time he was likely to show up at the gathering. Keeping people, especially Ghanaians waiting for hours at an event in the absence of a keynote speaker is always an eyesore. They may get hungry and upset and create for themselves, avenues to pose difficult questions to the President and be very unruly.

So, as a strategy, I was approached by the ambassador Pobee and her team to prepare a variety of dishes for quite a number of people. I said, "Ma don't worry, I'll take care of it." My wife and I prepared and delivered the dishes from our one and a half bedroom apartment. The auditorium was filled to capacity with an overflow to the lobby. In the absence of the President, we were signaled to serve the food and refresh our guests with some Ghanaian local beverages like the famous Bissap drink, *sobolo*, among other soft drinks and juices.

Till today, Ambassador Pobee continues to describe what happened that fateful Tuesday as a miracle. With reason being that, though the room was filled to capacity, every single person present at the gathering ate to their fill and we still had left over food enough to feed another set of guests. So, when the late President arrived at the auditorium it was all smiles, everyone was in a good mood. The late President in his best self shared a joke or two to diffuse any leftover tension and randomly selected from among the audience, a member of his National Democratic Congress (NDC) party to address all gathered. After his speech, the speaker, in a bid to hinder any representative from the then opposition New Patriotic Party (NPP) from taking a turn on the podium, proceeded to welcome the late President back on stage. *"No!"* exclaimed the president, *"I would like to hear from a member of the opposition party. If there's anyone here willing to speak, let them take their turn."* It was followed by thunderous applause and cheers for the late President. Of course, the food had done the trick but the late President set us all at ease with his charisma. In all, we had an amazing town hall meeting. no one misbehaved and there was nothing unruly in sight. Ghanaians had outdone themselves indeed!

Prior to serving the gathering at the auditorium downstairs, we saved some food for the President and his entourage in an executive style buffet setting upstairs in the conference room. Late President Mills however decided to have his share of the food brought to his suite at the Richmond Hotel in DC. Soon after the late President aired out his decisions, his entire entourage decided to follow suit with also having their food served at the hotel. Quickly, Ambassador Pobee asked me to go grab the food from the conference room to serve the President and his team as they had requested. By the time everyone downstairs had had second turns of the refreshments and slowly exited the space, I left Sarah in control at the main hall and followed late President Mills and his crew to serve at their hotel. So, this was where I had conversations and got up-close and personal with the late President, and also took the opportunity to properly introduce myself and get acquainted with him.

Ambassador Pobee was always kind enough to always introduce me to all the dignitaries who came knocking at the doors of the embassy. As part of the 'diplomacy' training I had personally received from her on the job, I came to appreciate that it was important for guests to pay their compliments to the chef at an event when he had cooked very well to meet or exceed their expectations. And as long as I was open to that kind of introduction, she made it happen with ease. As a top up to the compliments I'd receive, Ma, as I affectionately call her, would chip in this as a joke, "Francis takes his work too seriously." From over the years, Ma has become family, and I, her son. While she lived in DC, I'd go over every now and then to check on her, sometimes with my kids in tow for her to deliver to them, an unfiltered lecture on life and academics. 'Ma talk to them, I'm trying to get them to be like you. This one being lazy, this person isn't studying hard enough, the other is being that,' I'd go on and on and then she would say, "You see how mum and dad are working hard? You guys need to make them proud." Wherever in the world she was, I would track her down to check on her, be it on weekends or on festive occasions like Christmas. With very time spent in her presence, in every moment shared, she's never hesitant in telling me how well she thinks I have done for myself. Keeping my eyes on the ball, undeterred by those trials we all come across in our lives but soldering on and putting in my very best regardless of the circumstances. Every challenge she brought in my way, I excelled. Her late husband, Professor John Pobee who passed away in 2020, was like a father to me. He took his time to counsel me whenever I called on them. We would have deep conversations about life, work and any other topic worth discussing.

In 2015, when she again arrived in the United States from Pretoria to embrace her appointment as Ghana's permanent representative to the United Nations, she phoned me and said, "Francis, now that I'm back in DC, you will be helping me on this job. When I have to host the president whenever he's in town for the General Assembly, I can't think of anyone else to do the all catering for him and our over 300 expected guests." It implied that whenever there was a general assembly, I had to fly to New York to cater for the sitting President and other invited guests. In addition to serving wonderful meals from the time of former President John Dramani Mahama to the time of President Nana Addo Danquah Akuffo Addo, I took up the task of setting up all the tables and seeing to all floral arrangements.

When Otumfour Asantehene was invited by the United Nations to deliver a speech on September 13$^{th}$ 2019, at the UN's general assembly high level forum on the 25$^{th}$ anniversary of the adoption of the declaration and programme of action on a culture of peace, I was, again, called upon by the ambassador to cater for him and all invited guests. I had the pleasure of serving a cocktail formula I called the "Ashanti Mule," created the previous year at the Embassy Chef Challenge (ECC) as a dedication to the Asantehene Otumfour Osei Tutu II. The Ashanti mule is a combination of ginger drink mixed with *Kasapreko* gin and fresh mints. I served that as a cocktail alongside a buffet of Ghanaian and continental dishes. My evening was completed by the smiles on the faces of all who ate, drank and made merry at the reception.

In my years as a successful Chef and entrepreneur, I have to come to understand that, serving at occasions comprises of more than merely placing food on the table for all to see and eat. It is about how you go about your treats, presentations, floral arrangements, space setting and also incorporating certain unique table placements in your display which will be pleasing to the eye and also stimulate the appetite of your guests.

To stand out in your table settings, it is important to consider what makes you unique as an individual, your personal preferences and what defines you as a person. I usually go for my Ghana kente cloths or other unique fabrics or miniature wood carvings which screams "my motherland." A few other times, in a bid to showcase myself as if I were competing in a world class competition or simply to just elaborate more on my presentation, I'd go for an ice sculpture to display at the center of my table setting. When it came to food, even with the local Ghanaian snacks like *atwomo, nkate cake, agbele kaklo,* I carefully prepared and served them all with finesse without compromising on that authentic flavor. Simply put, it's all about creating a catering brand that people can trust and projecting yourself and business in the exact manner you want to be seen, received and appreciated by the world. I recall the first **Embassy Chef Challenge (ECC)** in March 2009, where I had the honor of competing with 27 chefs from various cultures in Washington D.C, which is the hub for over 180 embassies. With this competition a group of distinct chefs, highly regarded from their individual countries, converged under one roof to prepare authentic signature dishes and drinks of their home country. Ambassador Pobee, who was at the time the head of Chancery for the embassy of Ghana, gladly put me on to represent and project the image of Ghana out of a number of revered Ghanaian chefs in the Washington, Maryland and Virginia tri-state area.

The first day of the ECC, which is a month long celebration of

Washington D.C's diplomatic community, saw the wife of the then ambassador, Daniel Ohene Agyekum, and all other officers from the embassy were there to cheer and support me. Though I did not win any award or medal from competing that year and a couple of years after that, I still did not give up till I achieved the ultimate prize. After keenly competing in the previous years without any win, I improved on my beverage formula by creating the "Ashanti Mule" drink at the 2018 ECC as a dedication to the Asantehene Otumfour Osei Tutu II, where I bagged double honors that night. People's choice $2^{nd}$ Place, Judges choice $2^{nd}$ Place.

I presented the cocktail alongside black eyed peas and shrimp fritters, also known as *koose* as the starter and some good Ghanaian Jollof rice with lamb chops marinated in a blend of Ghanaian spices. In that same year, I also competed in the third annual **Grace Jamaican Jerk Festival** on June $10^{th}$ 2018 in Washington DC, which saw over 7,000 packed patrons on the lawns at the RFK stadium. I emerged overall best chef at the shoppers' celebrity chef Throwdown competition. In 2019 I, again, received the Pepsi best beverage $1^{st}$ place honors with a gold medal at the Embassy Chef challenge after participating every year since the onset of the ECC in 2009.

I was permanently in the books of the Ghanaian embassy as a staff and continued to hold my position as a supervisor at Maple wood Park Place. Yet, the desire to be more and do more came unquenched. The ECC afforded me the confidence and desire to partake in other competitive events. At the 2017 African cuisine Jollof festival, I emerged the overall best after keenly competing with highly renowned chefs from Nigeria, Thereby silencing the Jollof wars between Ghana and Nigeria. The trick, I believe, lies in being intentional in your step by step preparation of the meal, the thoughtful selection of organic spices and most importantly the quality of rice quantity of water used.

My skill as a chef, however, was not limited to the kitchen space, sometime in 2010, I found myself on Fox 5 D.C with Holly Morris, a revered news anchor and television host in the United States, where I tried to debunk the thinking that palm oil contained a high amount of cholesterol hence, bad for human health. Backed by good general and scientific research of course, I emphasized on its enormous health benefits including. Protecting against heart diseases, high in vitamin E an antioxidant which keeps the immune system healthy and to aid cells to communicate. Even in talking about that, I managed to hit on how it is excessively produced organically in Ghana, thereby creating a very good impression of my country. That interview created for me, an avenue to import and sell a number of bottles of organic palm oil made in Ghana in the United States. The delivery on TV was smooth this time, unlike the other day before the camera at GBC with all the first time jitters.

Oh yeah! With every opportunity comes a step to the next level. Ambassador Pobee once said in a conversation, *"In everything you need to work hard to justify the confidence placed in you. So, much as you are given opportunities, you have to take up the responsibility and work hard and shine through whatever platform you are given while working to overcome the anxieties that come with settling into a new space or embracing a new challenge."* Whose steps to better follow in this diplomatic space than hers? She has grappled with different challenges. Challenges of moving into a new setting, a new country, trying to live a normal life with family left behind — sacrificing moments forever lost to time.

*Apostle General Rev. Sam Korankye Ankrah, with his wife, Mama Rita Korankye Ankrah.*

*Hon. Alan Kyeremateng was always the kind to smile; Camera ready and always willing to meet you halfway in every decision. I must say that his rare humility rubbed off positively on me.*

*Just another evening at the Potomac residence with Hon. Alan Kyeremateng.*

*Ah! feast your eyes on these random photographs of my cheese cake and tropical fruit mousse. It is truly from moments like these that I derive joy... cooking and creating!*

*Ambassador Martha Pobee, Assistant UN Secretary- General for Africa and the woman who by the grace of God, single handedly ensured my welfare and permanent stay at the embassy of Ghana.*

*Ambassador Pobee, looking on with pride as I locked hands with Otumfour Osei Tutu II, the Asantehene of the Ashanti kingdom in Ghana, when he was invited to address the UN.*

*Ambassador Martha Pobee (left) and the head of chancery for Ghana's New York mission (right), after a dinner with the African community at the United Nations, When President Nana Addo Danquah Akuffo-Addo visited the mission.*

*With the former President of Ghana, John Agyekum Kuffour before our departure to West Virginia.*

*Chief Kuffour, the son of former President Kuffour, was present during our stay at the Greenbrier Hotel, West Virginia.*

*Some moments can never be forgotten; Priceless, rare. Such moments deserve a solo shot, to be framed for generations to see. Like this one with Otumfour Osei Tutu II.*

*Hilton Alexandria, 2006, with the late South African icon and Theologian, Desmond Mphilo Tutu.*

With the late former President of Ghana, John Evans Atta Mills on one of his visits to the embassy of Ghana in Washington.

For the clarity of this photo, blame the camera quality of the phone used. This was taken at the Potomac residence when former president Mahama visited during his time as vice President to the late John Evans Atta Mills.

*I still blame the quality of my phone's camera at the time… this photograph with former President John Dramani Mahama, still goes down as one of my favorites in my presidential archive.*

*The former mayor of Accra, Alfred Oko Vanderpuije, was also present at the Potomac residence.*

*Photographed with Mrs. Ernestina Naadu Mills, the wife of the late former President of Ghana, John Evans Atta Mills, at the Potomac residence.*

*2021 moments at the Royal house chapel in Maryland, USA, during a women's convention.*

*In every splendid culinary display lies the stress and creativity of a chef. The look on my face says it all.*

## STILLS FROM THE EMBASSY CHEF CHALLENGE (ECC)

*Ambassador Barfour Adjei-Barwuah, former Ghanaian ambassador to the USA, in talks with me after I presented the award from the ECC to him in Washington.*

## STILLS FROM THE GRACE JAMAICAN JERK FESTIVAL

*Remember when I wrote in the part two of this book that my wife and I complimented eachother in height? This is it! She stood beside me at the festival to accept the grand prize.*

In a pose with other competitor chefs after I had been crowned winner of the cooking contest.

President of Ghana, Nana Addo Danquah all smiles after presenting to him, the beverage of the day after the 76$^{th}$ UN General Assembly in 2021.

President Nana Addo Danquah Akuffo Addo at the table with Ambassador Martha Pobee and Ghana's Foreign Affairs minister, Shirley Ayorkor Botchwey at the 2021 UN General Assembly in New York.

# Part 4

# ...The Journey Continues

# Chapter 16

# Chapter 16

Sitting back on a cold Sunday night in the first week of November 2013, I solemnly replayed the struggles of the past to the stability of today. To unwind from the aches of the past week's activities, I sipped on a mug of hot chocolate while allowing my body to completely sink into the softness of the couch. "What's next?" I asked myself, watching my not-so-little daughter bring her brothers to order, as my wife paced about the entire square meter of the apartment, getting everyone to settle in for the night. My heart was full, yet, I still wondered about the next line of action for me and my family.
"Remember our conversation a week prior to catering for our church for the first time in the United States?" Sarah asked, interrupting my thoughts in the process.
"Erm, which of the conversations Payin? We engaged in several talks prior to that time o *anaa*?" It certainly would have been easier to have answered "No" to the question but it wasn't worth listening to a song on how 'men aren't always great listeners.'
"Look," she said, leaning over from behind with her hand lying gently on my shoulder, "Although you're be back on the Embassy's permanent staff list, you aren't in residency. Our business is, by the Grace of God, gradually picking up on the side. I believe it's about time went legit!"
"Legit?"
"Yes Joojo, It's about time we registered our business with the U.S government in order to spread our wings without fear."
Like an open book, Sarah could read me with ease. It was almost as if she were in my thoughts before the interruption. We were in

perfect sync. I figured it was a great idea, with Cecelia and her brothers going about their chores and school commutes independently, it indeed seemed like the perfect time to take our catering business to the next level. I took the liberty in discussing it with a few acquaintances, all Ghanaian, who in turn took the chance to discourage me from pursuing that goal. Per their view, all things were impossible to me due to my being an immigrant. They said, our dream to be a legitimate business, was best lived in our minds.

A naysayer cried, *"No No No, you'll be arrested when you go on with this. Do you really want to draw attention from the eyes of the government? They will be all on your case o.'* Another added, *"You are not a citizen o, so, don't even try."*

The Francis Otoo you have come to know is a go-getter. I like to take my chances in everything I put my mind to. Yet somehow, blinded by their views, I backed down in following through with it. The disappointment in my wife's eyes could not go unnoticed, so, in attempt to curb the situation before it escalated, I said, "well, if that's the case, let's do this small small. In sticking with catering for the church for now, I believe, we'll be met with greater opportunities."

Friends, the greatest deductions I derived from that situation was that, when God gives you a dream or a vision, YOU DO NOT, I repeat YOU DO NOT NEED TO CHECK WITH OTHERS FOR THEIR OPINION before pursuing. Because, your adversary the devil, who is always seeking to plant seeds of doubts and fear, will work through men to hold you back from stepping out boldly in faith to take over what belongs to you. As days progressed, our popularity increased within the Washington, Maryland, Virginia tri-state area. And as it increased, so did our orders. My wife and I decided that it was time to move out of our one and a half bedroom apartment into a much bigger space. "A three bedroom would do." she said. With the kids growing up so fast and Gilbert almost catching up to me in height, it would be best to settle into a space where everyone would have enough room to move about. We also looked out for an apartment with a kitchen, spacious enough to carry out our many orders without feeling suffocated. God had dealt wondrously with us indeed. Sarah and I could finally enjoy some privacy in our own home. our daughter could finally have her 'me' time away from the boys who then had to settle bed demarcation issues. Their actions were typical of my brother and me, in our early days at South Labadi Estates.

Wednesday, 29th June 2005, a few weeks after my children had settled in the United States, I recall taking further initiatives in settling the widening gap and make up for the lost times between my brother and me. I felt more estranged from my brother than ever. I believe it had to do with the all the complaints I had received from family and well wishers back home about his drinking habits and disappearing items from the house which he apparently sold to fund his habits. Whenever we got the chance to speak, I'd advise him to desist from the act but, I guess his emotional and physical dependency on the substance kept him going back. I had come to learn later on, that the burn in his throat which accompanied every sip he took, excited and solaced him. I personally found it bizarre that, two boys who grew up solely in the comfort of each other's company and in the absence of a father could have succumbed to the pressures of life to grow apart. It was, as a matter of fact that, in my quest to escape the tentacles of poverty, I had in a way given up on him.

I had spent over a year in America and had come to a conclusion to visit home without my family, just to spend some time with my brother for a change. I placed a call through to my brother to

catch up on lost times and to make up for the awkward ones in the past. It was a deafening silence after the first 'hello.'
"Joe, how have you been?" He started. Without waiting my response he proceeded to ask about Junior because he had taken a liking to him. Though Junior can't recall a single memory of his late uncle today, Sarah describes the intimate bond they both shared prior to moving to America as enviable. She had also grown to love Kwesi as her own. He was her 'second husband' after all.
Over the phone tried the hardest to sound like his usual bubbly self but, the breaks in his voice, the pauses in his breath after every word, gave him away.
"Joe if you're truly coming down this Christmas, do you mind bringing me a few things?'
"Oh Kwesi, should that even be a question? *wei dierr* you shouldn't have. Tell me what you'd like, *mjtc ama wo*." I replied.
"Oh *medaase*, thank you, I would like a wrist watch, shoes, T-shirt and any other souvenir you'd be willing to throw in as a bonus."

Together, we laughed at his response. It was refreshing to hear him list out specific material preferences without jumping straight for money as usual. We were finally making headway in our relationship. We laughed and joked like the old days at Grandma Maku's. My mood shifted for the better. The little boys who once played doctor and engineer with their plastic toys, had finally found their way back to each other. So, when the call regarding his demise came through three days later, I went completely numb. My legs tingled, everything hurt. It had been the most difficult part of my journey to embrace, till today. I continue to find it difficult to verbally share a memory of him to anyone without breaking into tears. As you have read, my father was nowhere near the premises of the funeral… that did not come as a surprise to me. The astonishing part was how he had gathered the 'courage', eleven years later, to fly all the way to the United States of America to reconcile with the son he had chased out of his home in cape coast.

I met **General Smith** after I had re-joined the Embassy of Ghana in 2009. I had heard about him when I lived at the 37 Military barracks with my mother. He happened to be a close associate of my dad from their years with the army. After a first introduction, he immediately made the connection and acknowledged me as indeed, the son of Rtd. Lt. Col Nicholas Otoo. He took me up as his son, introduced me to his wife who was quite accommodating. He was in the know about my accomplishments as a caterer in the United States and kept giving private reports to my father about how quickly "his son" had carved a niche for himself. He further admonished him to reconcile with me before it got too late. General Smith took the time to sit me down to apologize on my father's behalf. He recited all my father had done and coaxed me into forgiving him. *"I am an adult now. What he did to us rests with the past. I have forgiven him so let's let sleeping dogs lie."* I spoke.

I had no idea that He had already made the necessary arrangements and connections to bring my dad to physically render his apologies to me in the United States. Together, they came over to my house, in the absence of my children of course. There, my father began to narrate his remorse for not being there for us and how he would have gone back into time to make things right if he could. What about Kwesi? What about my mother? Didn't she deserve an apology as well? What If I had not been successful in my field overseas? Would he have seen the need to openly claim me as his son? These were among the many questions I asked myself while he spoke. Truth is, I was becoming quite blasé about all the apologies. I sat staring him eye-to-eye, to see if he truly meant his words. Somewhere in the middle of his statements, I drowned into series of unpleasant memories I experienced with him. I played back all jokes made by children in the hood about how we were fatherless, how school PTA meetings were a constant reminder that we were incomplete, how he looked me and my brother in the face before driving off our school premises with our step sister. And don't even get me started again on how he chased his whole adult son and Uncle out of his Cape coast home that sunny day, laying emphasis on how he had wanted nothing to do with us. What saddened my heart was knowing that Kwesi, who stood hand-in-hand with shame throughout the short span of his life, died without getting to see the 'remorse' of his father. Would he have forgiven him? I highly doubted that. So to wrap it up, I told him it was fine, and on behalf of my late brother and myself, I accepted his apology and let it go. It's still a sea of emotions whenever he comes to mind, so over the years, I have mastered the art of keeping that door shut. Time they say heals all things…let's see how that goes.

In our three bedroom apartment with our business steadily gaining popularity, I worried that Sarah might burn out from keeping up with her job and working multiple hours with me in meeting the rising demands of our clients. I even sat her down to talk her into quitting her nights and Saturday shifts to focus more on the business to save her some energy. But this woman, with a severe allergy to any form of idleness, even for a split second, convinced me with reasons why she was cut out for this and more. Our first child, Cecelia, stepped in to assist us in the cooking and setting up for church events and with the food packaging. Gilbert and Junior, if not at a weekend basketball game, would go with us to event locations as our personal assistants for the day.

Our daily activities brought us in the faces of people from all walks of life, Including a Jamaican who encouraged us to go on with the registering our business. After long hours of elaborating on how, according to my 'well informed' acquaintances, it was against the law for an immigrant to own a registered business. "How do you think we have a lot of Latin eateries nationwide. Aren't they immigrants as well?" He asked. It was the one question that shook me into reality. How did we not think of that? I guess we were too busy seeking council with the wrong circle.

While we were apprehensive about following up with an official business registration enquiry, we, however had the courage to go out in search for a kitchen in Bowie, Maryland. The evening before, Sarah and I had exhausted every Ounce of strength after catering for an elaborate wedding in Virginia. It was the wedding of an affluent couple in the Ghanaian community. After driving my entire family to the event premises in the minivan I had purchased after ditching the rickety plastic windowed car, we had spent 12 hours lifting and bending till the ceremony came to a close.

"*Awurade*! Are we truly about to clean up this apartment before turning in for the night?" Sarah asked in a groan. "*Eii* medeɜ mabrɜ o, I'm tired." Our children became our super heroes for the day. They helped out in taking the stress off Mummy and daddy. Like the old apartment, we had begun to outgrow our new place. The air was choked with the aroma of local and continental foods we had earlier prepared. As we kicked back the first hour of our arrival at home with a drink, and our aprons tossed somewhere over the kitchen counter, we figured it was time— again to move out. We combined a chunk of our individual savings to purchase a house we had closed on in Burtonsville, Maryland… our first home in America. We moved big in faith. The house in Burtonsville, Maryland had three bedrooms, a living room, a coat closet, a storeroom next to the wide airy kitchen and a spacious backyard. The upside of this purchase was that, we got to convert the backyard into an outdoor kitchen extension where we prepared and packaged all large orders. Orders like the wedding of the daughter of a Church of Pentecost elder, where my wife and I were tasked to prepare and serve an assortment of foods to over a thousand guests. Just the two of us, at the backyard, stood to prepare, from scratch to finish, every single order on the menu. The total number of calls kept rising every week. We were consistently booked for weddings, engagements, birthdays, graduation parties for an increasing number of guests. Right from the wedding of the daughter of the Pentecost elder, we noticed the tremendous change in our business. Our phones kept buzzing morning and night with calls and text messages coming in from Washington, New York, Virginia, all interested in booking Chef Francis and Sarah for their events. We were like one who dreamt. Our situation was turning for the better right before our very eyes. Would you believe me if I told you that some couples went as far as rescheduling their wedding dates just to fit in our schedule? Me, a South Labadi boy, now on the speed dial of the Americans.

"Let's make a move." I urged Sarah one evening. "Let's go and make all official enquiries ourselves to find out how we can begin the necessary steps towards legitimizing our business."
"And what if they turned us down?"
"So what if they turned us down?" I asked sharply. "If they do,

we would step aside and toss this out the window, knowing that we had at least put in some effort. And if they approve of us, glory be to God."

"I'm really liking your spirit today, but honestly I can't believe it took you over a year and a kind Jamaican to see things the right way," Sarah added.

She was right. It had taken up until November of 2014 to finally walk in the path I was supposed to have walked a year ago. Actually, the Jamaican was the agent we met in Bowie, Maryland while we were in search of a Kitchen for rent. He was in charge of the very first property we took an interest in. "Do you have a license?" he asked after directing us to his office in Baltimore for further discussions on the rental property.

"No we don't. We are currently looking into it." I replied.

"Sure."

"Sir, do you by any chance know of anyone who specializes in that area or could be of help?"

He smiled, "Actually, that's what I do."

My wife shook visibly in her seat. I, on the other hand, sat still with a stiff neck. We could not believe it. How could it all be coming together like that? There we were — the right place at the right time with the right person needed to facilitate the registration of our business beautifully ordained by God.

He continued, "I have been doing this for people for some years. It's quite easy. All I'll need is your I.D and your company name."

The Company name—we had given that a lot of thought. After crossing out a few ridiculous ones we had come up with, we decided to go with a portmanteau of our first names, Francis and Sarah. "FranSar". The agent thought it sounded good. So he run necessary checks on his application portal to make sure it was available. Since it was not taken by anyone, we were cleared and approved to use it. It cost about $600.00 to cover the entire process. After he requested that I followed him to an inner room to complete the process, I shouted, "We are not citizens o, we are immigrants."

"And who told you that you had to be citizens?" He replied in a thick Jamaican accent.

"You see?" Sarah cut in. "For over a year now, you have been scared to do an official follow up in aid of establishing your dream. Now, you see?"

"Why?" the agent asked almost bursting into laughter.

"Hmm," I answered, failing to develop and deliver a coherent thought.

Sarah went further to narrate how I had been discouraged by the counsel of my fellow Ghanaians which had deterred me from making these enquiries over a year ago. And that was when he questioned me on how I thought Spanish folks came about owning a lot of restaurants in America. "All you need is to rent or purchase a good kitchen, have it inspected and await approval from authorities. That's pretty much it." He concluded. That man was God sent. Though we had walked out of his office that noon without closing on the property, we left his office with a registered business in the Pipeline. The agent had filed the property we had wanted to purchase as our place of operation, took the $600.00 payment, said his congratulations and told us to wait on our certificates.

About 4 months into our encounter with the Jamaican agent, we continued to operate from our backyard kitchen extension without a license. In our daily lives, we went about business as usual: Embassy of Ghana, Maple wood Park Place, Hebrew Home, and Royalhouse Chapel, where I happened to be on the food /catering committee, and all other weekend/weekday catering contracts. I had married my buddy and my reflection, yet I believed that, the sole combination of our strengths could not have been enough to have made it that far. It had to be from the Lord. Years of working actively without ending up in the emergency room or getting put down for something as simple as a back or muscle ache was an absolute miracle. With every new day came the right amount of strength we needed to sail through.

Before our business certificates and license to operate were delivered two months later, we looked into advertising. We hired the services of a gentleman in Washington to create an official website for the business to help us reach a wider range of audience outside our tri-state area. We desired to have our business on a global platform. We placed ads in local newspapers. Printed and handed out some fliers to people we met on the street, at church and across the many streets in our neighborhood. We were ready. On the fliers we printed out our contact number and address, what we were about and what we specialized in. creating our official website, Fransarcateringservices.com, was the best decision of all. On the website we displayed vivid images of the variety of continental cuisines we prepared. West African, Asian, Middle Eastern, European, Caribbean and Mexican, with our Trademarked motto, *serving the world on a spoon since 1990*, in full glare. We operated from 9:00am – 05:00 pm on all weekdays and closed to general public on weekends to attend to booked events.

# Chapter 17

# Chapter 17

**June 15th 2015, Fransar Catering Services** was officially birthed while we still operated from home. A few weeks later, we finally rented a kitchen in Bowie, Maryland which was convenient to Baltimore, Washington Annapolis. From here, we operated as a Catering Service. Now, although Bowie, Prince George's county had low crime, affordable settlement and solid educational institutions, most temporal rentals in Bowie are not for the faint of hearts. Especially for wild dreamers like me, who visualized the perfect setting to operate and serve the many customers who showed admirable glances as they walked in to pick up their orders, or to make service reservations for impending events. The kitchen we settled on was one of the temporal commercial rentals which charged hourly for use. It was a feasible choice for startup catering business seeking to run large quantities of orders away from home at a centralized location, convenient to their target market. These temporal rentals provided glamorous and sophisticated spaces with available equipment to suit your every kitchen need, and help you relax as you carry out your tasks for the day. It had cabinets, Ovens, dishwasher, fridge, well aid flooring and countertops and chimneys to direct and remove all hot gases and smoke from your kitchen air. With illumination being a necessity in food preparation, these rentals provided a well lit space to see exactly what goes into your food. For those seeking to capture their cooking moments, it was definitely the go-to. There were options to choose from various kitchen styles and designs: U shape, L shape, A shape, a tiny or a huge kitchen... you only had the responsibility of selecting one that best suits your personality, and essentially the spatial requirement of your task at hand in order to perform without the need for extra room.

Now hear this, such rentals in Bowie are no pancake. We ended up paying $100.00 per hour to operate the business in this space, a simple recipe for failure. Perhaps it was the undying need to succeed. The sheer excitement to see me live out a boyhood dream, the idea of operating separately from home in an equally sophisticated space, I feel, conferred on me a feigned sense of importance. I had developed the notion that all, who patronized our services, would be willing to offer more if they were received in a sophisticated space. *"We'll make our money back in no time,"* I thought. In the locked coffers of my mind, I kept the "well structured" plan with the expected profits I had already taken the liberty to make further plans with. Yes, presentation matters with every catering business, but I could have opted for a less expensive space with an equal level of sophistication without milking the team dry. The lesson there was to simply not count my chickens before they hatched. Busily making plans on profits from monies yet to be received is a sure way to quickly fold up a small business.

Fransar in Bowie was a disaster. We could not break even. Though the loss was weighty, I kept going because throwing in the towel was out of the plan. No, failure was an option I could not settle for. We had realized, a few months later that, we had invested all our earnings from other avenues into keeping the Bowie kitchen dream running. Though we had focused on creating the best meals to attract more customers and had made good sales, we couldn't earn higher than the total amount of all we had invested into the hourly rental payment. The next logical step was to move. It was highly unlikely to stumble upon an affordable rental without any lead so we hired the services of an agent who, by God's Grace, found one in Gaithersburg also in Washington DC. Gaithersburg was about 25 minutes away from our home in Burtonsville. We had again, moved back to cooking from our backyard as Bowie rentals kept escalating. Our neighbors, though understanding, I believed had had enough of the clanking of pots and pans plus the aroma that constantly swept through the air. We needed to move, and it had to be soon. With the immense assistance of an agent, we found a well crafted kitchen which went for $30.00 an hour. That's $70.00 in savings. We only had to drive about 25 minutes every day from Burtonsville to Gaithersburg to prepare and package orders for the day and take on other bookings for the week. We turned a spare room in our Burtonsville home into an office where, business records were kept along with event planning and clientele meetings were sometimes held.

We, at Fransar catering, were full service caterers who cooked, delivered, set-up venues and served at all events. On a typical day for Fransar, we worked tirelessly with our clients to plan and create menus to suit their style, most importantly dietary needs and taste. We created contracts for clients to facilitate a smooth transaction of business. Aside setting up tables at event centers, we sometimes hired on extra helping hands to serve food, clean up and tear down the dining area after the close of day. additionally, we had a running daily menu where we sold single packages of food to our clients who were permitted to either pick up or opt for a courier service to pick up for delivery. We carried on with catering for funerals, weddings, parties etc. while I continued to cater for the Embassy's Independence Day celebration and all Holiday parties. The Francis Otoo brand kept growing.

A true caterer, I have come to comprehend over my fifteen years of being in the catering industry, is not one with great cooking skills only. It is, however, one with excellent customer service and strong leadership skills. He or she must possess the ability to come up with different menus and have knowledge in dietary restrictions. He or she should also be able and willing to hold conversations with clients, guests and all permanent and temporal employees. Observing my activities in the industry, it is safe for me to say that these have contributed to my ability in creating a trustworthy brand over the past years. It is with these tools or qualities that Sarah and I have molded Fransar Catering Services. Even when we serve Ghanaian and all other West African cuisines, we try to add a little bit class to it and portray them in such a way that Non-Africans could patronize.

When I initially became a personal chef of Rev. Sam Korankye Ankrah, I didn't quite know if it was going to stick or be on a long term basis. I had picked up the honor years after I had relocated to the United States. I flew in occasionally to Ghana Whenever the Apostle requested for my services, including the wedding of first and only son, **Paapa Korankye Ankrah in December 2014.** I stayed in Ghana throughout the entire wedding celebration which, including all preparations lasted a week. Paapa and his sweetheart, whom he met on his pursuit of knowledge in the United Kingdom, were set to be joined in Holy matrimony at the Oil Dome of the Royalhouse Chapel International, Ahenfie in Accra, Ghana.

The wedding which was adjudged the 2014 wedding of the year was graced by the presence of powerful men and women of God like. Bishop Dag Heward-Mills, founding Bishop of the lighthouse chapel International and his wife Adelaide Heward-Mills. Bishop Charles Agyin Asare, Presiding Bishop of the Perez Chapel International. Dr. Opoku Onyinah, Chairman of the Pentecostal council. Mama Christy Doe Tetteh of Solid Rock Chapel, Bishop Dominic Allotey, founder and General overseer of Living Faith International church in New York, among other reputable men of God were all present to show love to Reverend Sam Korankye Ankrah and his family.

I was tasked with the honor of catering for all dignitaries and other attendees present, numbering to over 3,000 people. I, by the Grace of God, was able to single-handedly create and serve a menu of local and international dishes, with all manner of proteins and vegetables at beautiful buffet set up. It was one of the greatest challenges ever picked up in career as a chef. 3,000 guests — that figure was more than enough to set even the greatest of all chefs off into fear and trepidation. Three square meals comprising of various assorted rice, vegetables, and desserts. It would be completely hypocritical to deny the fact that I did have some jitters throughout the period of celebration. I melted into a heap of calm after some guests sent in their compliments, and the Apostle gave a pat on my shoulder. It had all worked out in the end. Aside Paapa's wedding. I flew to Ghana on the occasion of the Apostle's 50th and 60th birthday to cater for each celebration. To the glory of God, My cooking has become an integral part of major celebrations in the household and office of the Apostle.

Serving the Apostle General over the years, I had come to learn to adjust my cooking to his taste and tailor his nutritional needs to every bite. Knowing he was somewhat a pescatarian in his diet, I needed to create fun and enjoyable dishes to give him something to look forward to at the table. Whether it was sheet pan Salmon, stuffed shrimps, smoked Salmon, baked cod, grilled garlic butter shrimps, or ginger scallion steamed fish. I ensured that they were served with vibrant colours and an assortment of vegetables. With my knowledge of dietary restrictions and nutritional needs, I made available to him a variety of tasty vegetables to accompany his main meal at every table sitting. It was all geared towards not making burdensome, the idea of consuming vegetables.

Raised to become typical Ghanaians like we are, we were trained to solely depend on heavy carbohydrate diets for survival. Breakfast for a typical Ghanaian was mainly *Hausa koko* and *koose*. The *koko* was porridge made from millet and the *koose*, fritters made from a mixture of black-eyed peas and flour. For lunch, Ghanaians would have their *kenkey*, made entirely from corn, and often accompanied by fish and grounded pepper. Others go for *fufu*, which is a starchy blend of pounded cassava and plantain. As for supper, oh! Trust my fellow Ghanaian to sit to some *banku* with pepper or okra stew–all carbohydrate! It was much later in our adult lives that we discovered how our bodies demanded a lot of fruits and vegetables to flush out toxins and function properly. And with my expertise and knowledge, I have managed to make the transition delightful for every Ghanaian I have worked with. From their faces, you could always tell when the clouds of their earlier perceptions of consuming vegetables had lifted. I have, over the years, grown from ordinarily meeting the nutritional needs of the Apostle to becoming a son–a spiritual son, through true selflessness, kingdom mindedness. I can't seem to comprehend why he delights in eating my meals above all others, yet I believe that there are varying levels of Grace at play over every man.

As members of the food committee of the Royalhouse Chapel in Maryland, USA, My wife and I have been committed over the past two decades of our lives and career, to serving the church with our contributions and presence since departing the shores of Ghana. We have had the honour of being tasked with catering for guests from different nations who fly in daily to attend the various annual conventions organized by the administrative body of the church. To New York or whichever state the conventions were to be held in, I would fly in to perform the duties expected of me. Of course there was always the issue of unforeseen circumstances and inconveniences, and in such situations where I was unable to represent, I would get on phone to with the chef in charge, to coach and counsel on what and how things needed to be presented and presented.

The mission of sharing my knowledge has always been a selfless one. Reflecting on struggles of the past has created for me, a nature of constantly needing to see young people win. By sharing and imparting knowledge acquired from the school of life, I get to secure my position as the first cheerleader of whoever my path crosses with. There is something satisfying in every second spent, helping to steer the career of up-and-coming catering enthusiasts who have the desire to leave a mark in the hall of fame. For instance, I would get on the phone with the resident chef of the Apostle General every week, giving guidance on whatever meal or dish he would like to try his hands on. It could be likened to practical distance learning and tuition.

Fransar Catering Services continues to serve the world on a spoon to people from all walks of life. For the past seven years, we have and continue to cater to notable people and dignified events in and out of the United States. Including the wedding of Alexander Kyeremateng, son of Hon. Alan Kojo Kyeremateng in Washington. the annual UN General assembly in New York for the African community, Royalhouse in Maryland, USA, The Nigerian embassy, The Sierra Leonean embassy, African Union, African weddings and also for my friends at the US state department where we served a buffet of cuisines from all around the world.

In 2021, when Otumfour Asantehene celebrated the Akwasidae in the United States on August 8th in Maryland, Fransar catering was called upon to cater for the entire occasion. The Asantehene who happened to be in the USA after observing the Awukudae style in Ghana three months earlier decided to hold a durbar in Rockville, the seat of Montgomery County, Maryland. Otumfour sat in state to observe the day with the Asanteman community in the US.

It was a colourful ceremony which saw all attended clad in beautiful *Kente* cloths, an emblem of the Akan culture and tradition. The drummers also clad in kente and other traditional fabrics played the *'kete'* while a section of the attendees got on the dance floor to exhibit their dance skills. The magnificent celebration is centred on ancestral reverence, celebrating and recognizing past kings of the Ashanti kingdom of Ghana. The Akwasidae, celebrated every six weeks a year, captures the splendour and rich culture of the Asanteman. The spiritual rallies with the physical on every Akwasidae, centralising on ancestral worship as the leaders of Manhyia call upon the spirits of past kings to invoke their blessings on the Ashanti people. On the day before the Akwasidae, which is *Memeneda dapaah*, royal elderly women of Manhyia sing songs to the palace grounds to set the festival in motion. They drum to invite the spirits of the dead, they dance to welcome the spirit of these past kings who are expected to shower their blessings on their people by the end of the celebration. My wife and I served in amusement, observing the beautiful Ghanaian culture on full display. Outside of the drumming and dancing, I had come to learn at the event grounds about the solemn part of the Akwasidae, which included rituals to eulogize the serving King and presenting sacrifices to the ancestral spirits. It also involved the purification of ancestral hand-carved stools which are positioned on a podium to allow the Asantehene, sub-kings and elders to pay homage. A ram is sacrificed with its blood and insides smeared all over the stools as a means to revive the ancestral spirits. I believe these essential solemn parts were carried out in Ghana to allow the celebration to be observed by the Asantehene in Maryland.

The menu of the day was simple. We created an 'Asanteman' inspired dishes where we prepared a variety of local soups including *abunuabunu,* which is prepared from cocoyam leaves popularly known as *kontomire* and is served with snails and dried fish. we also had *werewere nkwan,* which is a soup prepared from melon seeds which are excellent sources of proteins, folate, thiamine, vitamin B6, zinc, iron. also available were goat light soup, chicken light soup.

For stews we served simple vegetable stew, Ghanaian black pepper stew (shito), beans stew, chicken stew, beef stew which paired excellently with white rice, *banku,* boiled yam and plantain. We also had *mportomportor* (yam pottage), *apapransa* , made from roasted corn flour and palm nut soup, etor (mashed yam or plantain often served with boiled eggs and peanuts). The celebration was climaxed with performances from an Ashanti performance troupe based in the state of Maryland.

# Chapter 18

# Chapter 18

**A MERRY OTOO CHRISTMAS - 2021**
25th December each year to me was an avenue to work for the extra cash. I know, Francis barely took a breather. To my boys, it was an opportunity to receive new video games or whatever item they had deliberately hammered on in the past months. Ceci had the look of simply being grateful to be home with family and commemorating the occasion with a full house of her favourite people. Christmas of 2021 was scheduled by the rest of the family to be different. Sarah did not think it was going to be so easy to get me to sit in that year with the family rather than go about my yearly pursuit of occasions to cater for during the festive season.

The pie Sarah carried from the kitchen was steaming and savoury. She remains the only person apart from a very good restaurant or myself whom I am comfortable enough to eat from. My face brightened when she placed the pie at the centre of the dining table. It was an apple pie — the kind I liked. From upstairs, the kids could be heard giggling and speaking on top of their voices. Kids? Let me not kid myself. These were no longer interested in hugs and kisses from their parents or something as simple as fixing their hair for them. They were two men and a woman now. Cecelia, aside from her academic prowess, was already killing it in the Fransar kitchen. On vacations and weekends, she took up administrative, managerial and cuisine duties with her parents. It made Sarah glad that one of our children had taken up an interest in the family business.

The suitable silence which characterized our home had perished with Christmas Eve. They had it all planned, my wife and kids. the matching Christmas comfy costumes and Santa hats. I could not have seen that coming. "Do I need to change into this outfit before sitting?" I asked with concern after pulling out the red and green onesie from its bag. It was one for adults and I certainly was unsure I had mentally prepared my mind to fully embrace the uniformed spectacle. "No costume, No food!" the response they gave, which had appeared almost rehearsed was enough persuasion to get me to go upstairs to change. It wasn't all bad–the costume. It was comfortable. Against my skin, it felt like a mother's hug — warm and cosy. We had a well-lit Christmas tree in our living room, which we had adorned with all colours of balls, bells, stars and a ceramic baby Jesus. Beneath the tree, we placed our wrapped gifts for one another with Christmas cards filled with words we barely told ourselves on a regular day. The Otoos dropped their guards and showed a level of vulnerability openly to one another on that day. It was beautiful. I lived one of the many reveries I had while I was camped at the AAMAs in Kokrobite in Ghana. I lived in a family where I got to be present as a father for boys, breaking what could have easily become a generational curse.

"No more please," I said gently pushing the bowl of mashed potatoes towards Sarah. The perfect opportunity to get me to eat had presented itself and she was not going to back down. If I knew Sarah, it was her chance to give me a possible spoon-feeding session if hadn't cleared my plate clean.

As an Executive chef working all manner of jobs till late in the evening, there was barely time to sit for a proper meal. Mine was to cook and watch others enjoy. The most I did was do a little decent tasting after the presentation or enjoy one of Sarah's packaged sandwiches or soups in the car en route to another job. This has been my life for the past two decades. The boys ate heavily while they shared stories from college. Yes, college. How did the time go by that fast? The word sounded new whenever it was mentioned. It felt like I was hearing that they were already in college for the very first time. I shared a story or two about Christmas in South Labadi, when my affluent cousins and Aunty shared *"aburokyire"* toffees and biscuits and some of their good hand-me-downs. I went on for minutes about how we came about all kinds of fireworks Ghanaians affectionately called "knock-outs" to disturb the entire neighbourhood. We stole some coins from Grandma Maku's purse to sponsor our purchases and that of our friends. The signature Christmas meal then was anything with chicken. Chicken was the constant in all Christmas meals in South Labadi: Fufu with chicken light soup, rice with tomato stew and chicken or Jollof rice with fried chicken. It was only in *Adukwei's* house that I smelt the aroma of goat light soup. He was one of the boys we played with. Ben did not like him that much because they seemed well-to-do than the rest of us. He couldn't make sense of his desperation to associate himself with the likes of us. After the usual 25th Christmas church service, Ben and I went house to house seeking food and gifts. We ate at almost every stop we made. With our *kwashiorkor looking* bellies and a pocket full of assorted candies and biscuits, we would go home as happy boys who had lived the day to its fullness. My kids could not relate... thank God. Wasn't that what I had prayed and toiled hard for? They looked on in awe, wondering how we were able to live through the struggle without indulging in vices for an easy way out.

We prepared for the Christmas service at the Royalhouse Chapel International, where we sat for sermons from Apostle Emmanuel Agormeda and other invited speakers. The significance of the birth of our saviour was re-introduced to us with an admonishing to live righteously. As I looked over the rows ahead, I realized how the space was filled with families. Some mixed and matched their colours to make a statement that they belonged together. Some church mothers wore their signature church crowns which I believed differed according to their personalities. the bolder the person, the more elaborate the hat. Sarah had a few of those she wore with amazing grace, they all did. Those hats were synonymous with Sunday service but because it was Christmas, it was bound to make an appearance in the house of worship.

At home, I helped my wife in the kitchen to put lunch together. We decided to give the kids a touch of Ghana and our childhood. My childhood. We made ready a bowl of chicken groundnut soup with rice balls. I used to enjoy the burnt part of the rice moulded into balls to enjoy with soup. We called it *"emutuo kanzo."* They enjoyed it. It was a joy to share a piece of Christmas from my childhood. There came a video call from my eighty-year-old mother, who didn't look a day over sixty. Rtd. Lt. Col Victoria Larko Abadji had grown to become my confidante. As her only living child, I owed it to her to support and take care of her till her dying breath. Loneliness was one thing I made sure would not engulf her. From the corners of her milky eyes, you could see the undiluted joy and feeling of gratitude to see us all together in one space. It was all she wanted for me...stability and that was what she saw. "When are coming to take me to America?" she asked her grandchildren. "Soon Grandma, how about next year?" the children asked. It was an expected response because it had become almost a pleasantry they shared on every occasion. *"I have moved into the oyarifa house now. The mango trees have grown bigger. I can't tell which type they are but the fruits are quite huge, and the oranges fruit all year. Joojo, I also asked the construction workers to go on a hiatus. It is Christmas and they should be with their families."* Ma enjoyed talking about everything. It was what I liked about her. I looked forward to her Christmas calls. It was a summary of discussions we've had, tackled and discussed all year. It ranged from politics, religion, the kids' academic performances, Sarah's well-being and if I was being present as a father and a good husband to her. Ma was a good Ma. The kids showed her images of the onesies we had all rocked earlier before church which made her laugh so hard. *"So you got our taller to wear this Christmas jumpsuit? How did you do it because when he was a little boy, he found these outfits disgusting?"* she asked Sarah. Not much to my surprise, I had ended up becoming the end of a well-crafted joke of the season. All the same, it felt good to see my mother and wife smile, my kids living the life I wished I had when I had attained their age.

*You do not choose your family. They are God's gifts to you as you are to them.*
- *Desmond Tutu.*

The strength of a family, I have come to believe, lies in the ability to make the heart of each other smile, to lighten the load and burdens of feeling alone and incapable. It is the source of identity and confidence for an individual. In the absence of a complete unit, I grew up questioning who I was, and to an extent, my capabilities. God, in all His all-knowing ways, planted each and every one of us among the group of people we get to identify with.

To be able to fully function in the food ministry, He knew that I needed to be placed in a family whose central dynamic was all about catering. One whose matriarch delighted to impart the skill of cooking to all who came after her. To her, it was a legacy she intended on keeping alive even after her passing. Being a part of this family, I had front-row seats to be taught every skill associated with West African cuisine. It was the booster I needed to embrace my calling and true purpose. The challenges I was posed along the way, I believe were a learning bonus to become skilled at effectively managing finances and time, and how to be accommodating to the ever-evolving personalities and attitudes of human beings.

By the end of the evening, after all the photographs, church service, calls and laughter were done, the Otoo 5 sat again to say grace and enjoy some chicken and rice. The exact order of Christmas meals I had back home in Ghana. We turned our living room into a cinema, where we all sat to enjoy some trending seasonal movies on Netflix. That felt nice. All five of us were seated and settled in to spend the night away. One-by-one, the kids said their goodnights and went upstairs to their rooms to probably get on their phones to see what their friends had been up to on Whatsapp or Instagram. Sarah slept off before the movie was over. About forty-five minutes into the 2-hour movie, she had gone silent on my left shoulder. She's usually the type to ask questions — I mean a lot of questions throughout a movie. The activities of the day had worn her out. The one day away from Fransar and our usual jobs, she gave in to sleep with ease. It was satisfying to see her relaxed for a change. In our minds, we both knew that $26^{th}$ December was another day with many reasons and opportunities to slide back into our 'normalcy.' With every idle minute spent before the television in the living room with my wife in my arms, I got to relax and reflect on how glorious of a day it had been... the one Christmas to remember.

# Chapter 19

# Chapter 19

**THE TIME WE TOOK A BREAK**
"This is a breathtaking view Joojo. I wonder why it took us this long." Sarah said standing by the giant glass windows, her silhouetted figure shone in full display through her flowing flowery summer dress. I stood up from the bed, inched her up against the glass window, grabbed her lower body from behind the waist and planted a soft kiss on her shoulder. With that, Sarah and I looked out into the vista – a vast gorgeous landscape comprising soft breeze, lavish greenery on the side sitting a few meters away from the shoreline and the rising of a golden sun.

In all the years we had been together, two years of dating and over a decade of marriage, it was the very first-time Joojo and Sarah had taken time for themselves away from the bustles of their normalcy as partners of FranSar. I knew that I had wanted her from when I first set eyes on her, Sarah, but, if anyone had told me that we would be tied at the hips in all of our endeavours throughout the years, I would have highly doubted that. Yet there we were, two lovers, partners, co-owners and parents, giving ourselves the much-required leisure together. Celebrating the fruits of our hard work and love, happy years of our adult working lives.

They say it is located where 'Connecticut meets the shore'. The Water's Edge Resort. It has been in service for over thirty years, accommodating and treating locals and tourists with fine services at its beautiful character residences and private beach.

With the ocean in view, the establishment maintains its charm as its building complex has been designed to take advantage of the scenery. The resort had 4 restaurants comprising a little café and authentic Italian restaurants. It is equipped with a beachside pool, a majestic spa and a myriad of entertainment options. The setting with its distinct character creates lasting memories. This white sand resort had kept and continues to keep its image as a top New England beachfront resort for vacations and getaways. Acres of grounds overlooking the water, a private beach area, this is where Connecticut goes to find the shore. The evening dinners were spectacular with views of the water and large patios – the perfect space to sip and savour. The staffs were pleasant and always ready to assist all who called upon them. For the first vacation as a couple, we could not have made a better choice. The sounds of the rushing ocean waves at night and the stillness of the water in the light of day were all I didn't know I needed. There's a calm to everything about water, as one with a hyperactive mind, the *swoosh swoosh* sounds of the ocean every minute gave me something else to focus on rather than the "what next" and "what ifs" of life and career. About twice a month, the resort held live band performances on one of the large patios over the water view. Luckily, we happened to have lodged at the premises on one of their live band weekends.

The resort was situated specifically in Westbrook, which was pretty much a small town in the 1900s. The 14-acre Water's Edge Resort began as a summer beach cottage for a family from New York. After the 'great depression' apparently took its toll on this family, the property was sold in 1940 to one Bill Hahn and his sister Ruth. Guest houses were erected, a greenhouse and even a movie theatre. The hotel could accommodate 400 guests on busy summer nights. It soon became a hub for Hollywood stars, musicians, artists and celebrities. After Bill Hahn passed, the establishment crumbled to bits and deteriorated. Along came Michael Dattilo, a real estate developer from Spring Valley who purchased what had remained of the once A-list establishment, replaced and repaired several buildings and eventually, the resort at which we melted away our stress, Water's Edge Resort and Spa was open, A true reflection of rich history. Thanks to the on-site brochures and the little checks I had run on the internet before embarking on what would become a priceless archive of memories.

Our villa was one of the 20 by the sea. The resort had 97 rooms at the main hotel and 68 condos, all created on distinct parts of the vast acre of property. The villa by the sea seemed like the perfect choice for the level of relaxation we looked

Forward to. I recall it was a whole month of intense back-to-back events. We were super booked and busy with a tall list of events on Fransar's calendar and we still had to ensure we made it on time for our jobs, mine at Maple Wood Park Place and Sarah's at the Hebrew Home. It was a crazy month. I recall Sarah hammering on her stiffening muscles and pounding migraines. Me, I was drained… just drained of all energy having made little to no time for sleep. Thank God for Instagram 'discover feeds' where you're exposed to random posts from people all over the world. That's how we discovered, our sanctuary, away from life, work and the increasing demands of our time. The serenity we found at the Water's Edge resort in Westbrook, Connecticut, availed us the opportunity to rekindle our bond and be alone, together.

My wife's favourite spot was the spa. I find it baffling how one could simply find rest or even pleasure in having hot mud or steam poured and blown onto their face. Yet somehow, that worked for Sarah. The feet and full body massage I could agree because our jobs required a lot of standing. To be able to keep serving people, we had to present the best of ourselves in the best of moods and an achy body could deny us the pleasure of serving wholeheartedly. My nerves were elated with our decision to take a break. I could tell from how less they tingled that, they were in a good place. The sounds of *oohs* and *aahs* freely flowing out of our mouths in harmony were enough signs to say that spa was a terrific idea. The Bible, even, admonishes us to take a sabbatical once every week. Remember the Sabbath day and keep it holy, (Exodus 20:8), the word also encourages us to keep, our minds, body and soul balanced. in proverbs 11:1, the Bible says that a *false balance is an abomination to the Lord: but a just weight is His delight*. Each soul has an assignment, a task to complete and report to the creator on the last day. However, the soul, without the body, a healthy one, cannot fully operate in the human world. Overworking our vessels without taking the needed break is a sure way to fast-track our journey to the grave.

Intentional rest is an exhibition of our trust in God's supremacy and power over our lives. It is letting go of the need to constantly control every happening in our lives. The world won't stop revolving, yes time will go by, but it is up to us to trust that God will keep for us what's ours as we allow our bodies to heal from all the damages and inflammations created from the pressures of life and various pursuits of success. It is, in fact, a demonstration of our humility and ability to truly let go

And let God align new things and opportunities for us as we honour the necessary sabbaticals in our lives. The getaway afforded me the space to get closer to my maker, develop new Bible study plans and plant some seeds of Grace, love, peace and joy. It is how I understand and value the aforementioned scripture I, proverb 11:1, that a false balance is an abomination to the Lord.

On our second night, which happened to be on a Friday, we joined other workaholics to end the working week and usher in the good weekend, with some queen-cut prime ribs, roasted potatoes and vegetables at the seafood bistro. Sitting at the table, enjoying the chunk of well-cooked protein, while succumbing to the feel of the chilly sea breeze on our skin as we watched the sun — slowly seeming to sink into the clouds gathered behind the ocean — was truly refreshing. I called "dining to sunset," Absolutely breathtaking. Sarah smiled a lot. Seeing new people, breaking away from the boredom in the routine of our daily lives, letting her hair down to breathe and sip on a chilled glass of champagne. With her phone on silent mode, I observed how she continued to settle into the space of doing absolutely nothing but relaxing and being taken care of for a change.

At about 7 pm that same evening, we walked to the sunset bar and grill also within the premises of the resort to enjoy some quality and soothing live band music from a trio, whose name I fail to recall. It screamed class and elegance. live music in a proper setting by the ocean. We joined other couples on the floor to dance to tunes from the trio, which I described by the end of the evening as Connecticut's finest. She was no better dancer than I was, Sarah. I had teased that she only moved one leg up and down three times before switching to the other leg to repeat. She accompanied those leg movements with snapping fingers, moving hips, hand claps and head nods. She was saved when the band switched to a slower tune to commence the slow dance session for the night. It reminded us of our first dance together as a couple on our wedding day.

*Yes, you're lovely, with your smile so warm and cheeks so soft.*
*There is nothing for me but to love you*
*and the way you look tonight.*
*With each word, your tenderness grows*
*tearing my fear apart*
*and that laugh that wrinkles your nose*
*touches my foolish heart*
*lovely, never, never change*
*keep that breathless charm*
*won't you please arrange it?*
*cause I love you*
*A-just the way you look tonight.*

With each line, the lead singer effortlessly sang *the way you look tonight*, almost as if the original singer Tony Bennett or even Frank Sinatra was there. Sarah wore a thin strapped black sequined ankle-length dress with a silky soft scarf over her shoulder. Holding my lady so close with my eyes closed, I inhaled the fragrance of her favourite 'Pure poison by Christian Dior' in her and on her neck. I reeled in every second of peace and acknowledged how far we had come in life and love. It was God's doing.

On Saturday, after Sarah's facials and my time at the sauna, I treated my queen and myself to an evening of fine piano dining at the Dattilo restaurant. As a chef, it's never a painless thing to sit and enjoy the meal. With every bite, my brain actively works to figure out which spices were used, and how long whatever we ate was grilled, roasted, boiled or baked. At the table, I quickly switched from discussing politics to trying to get Sarah to analyze and rate the cooking we were served, there was no 'off-switch' to that part of me.

We took a walk at the beach after the fine piano dining. At first, it was a way to walk in the fullness of our bellies but we ended up re-living our days as young lovers on a Saturday at the Labadi beach. The short strong wind ruffled her hair and nearly blew the wide cashmere scarf she had left hanging across her shoulder away. We felt young again. We laughed and even discussed retirement plans and fun activities to incorporate. Water's Edge had given us real value for every penny we spent at their premises. We had the next 24 hours to rest and sit idly at our sea view villa before being chauffeured to the airport for our 47-minute flight back to Maryland. Our plan to rejuvenate our bodies had worked perfectly. The 2017 summer visit to the Water's Edge Resort was the first of many vacation spots we continued to visit after Sarah and I had agreed to incorporate an active vacation schedule into our annual calendar.

In 2018, we did visit Connecticut again, this time it was to the Winvian Farm Cottages in the Litchfield Hills. Sarah was sure to settle on a resort with a spa and Winvian made the cut. This distinct holiday destination was supported by the fine-dining restaurant which was only known as 'The Restaurant.' The farm included unique cottages, each with their own individual character. One could choose from a wide range of fun options including camping, golfing, and enjoying the bird-view from the farm's fun and stylish chopper. The quiet getaway sat on 113 acres, surrounded by extensive woods and lakes. The farm was without a doubt, created to recharge its visitors. Like it says in their brochure, *"Winvian farm aspires to host you with no airs but graces, no extravagance or opulence, only warmth and treats."* The farm had a tree house, a pool and a range of farm activities to do in the Litchfield Hills of Connecticut, including fishing and horseback riding. The woods were leafy, lovely and thick, all great for hiking and other wild forest adventures. The atmosphere allowed for hot air ballooning and countless simple pleasures like canoeing on the river, playing tennis and golfing on the course, volleyball and bocce ball.

The spa was a realm of stillness, all 5,000 square feet of it. The knots in our muscles began melting away as soon as we walked through the doors —again for a couple's massage. We arrived at the hotel at about 11 am and made our way to the spa at about 3 pm for an hour of pure bliss. Full body massage sessions with a range of restorative treatments and therapies. We were offered cups of organic tea at the open lounge overlooking the green leafy woods. The birds, each one of them, chirped in varying tunes signalling the end of another day. What a great way to kick start our 3-day vacation! I spotted the sauna at the end of the hall. Perhaps I could sit again, stewing in minutes of my body sweat and steam from wherever it emerged, after my subsequent day of golfing. I had it all planned... get all dressed in my sportsman apparel and go golfing in the greens, while Sarah indulged in whatever she had planned for that morning after breakfast. We had the remainder of the day to explore the rest of Winvian farm, their entertainment and most importantly their cuisine together.

The cottages, all luxury accommodations, at the farm were nestled into the neighbouring woodlands. The accommodation was categorized into about 19 distinct cottages with unique details and make-up. I recall the artist colony cottage, which I believe was created for introverted people with a taste for imaginative or creative painting. I could tell because of the easels, and canvas paints inside the separate studio in the cottage. The artist colony cottage was an arts and crafts bungalow, comprising three airy rooms, a romantic bathtub and a painting studio, all connected by arched doorways. It was beautiful alright but not for the likes of my wife and I. there was also the beaver lodge, the Charter Oak, camping cottage, Connecticut Yankee, Golf cottage, Greenhouse, Hadley suite, Helicopter Suite, industry suite Library style suite, Log cabin suite, Maritime suite, secret society cottage, stable, stone style (its entrance looked almost like in Flintstones animation), Tree house and Woodlands cottage.

Sarah and I chose the Resort Cottage Rhapsody. The harmonious escape was tucked into the woods. The windows were floor-to-ceiling with a well-lit space. we even had a fireplace in the bedroom, which had a king-sized bed. With the touch of a button, the drapes slowly sealed off the rooms to allow for some privacy. The jetted soaking tub and rainfall shower head bathing space, played music of their own. The windowed glass door opened into the woods of Connecticut, providing you with the perfect greenwood view as you soak your stress away in the fragranced and salt bath in the tub.

I found Sarah seated at the front porch of the cottage upon my return from the golf course that morning, she had a glass of fresh juice and a magazine in hand. I did not play like a pro, not even halfway to becoming a pro but I knew I had swung hard enough to earn myself a short time with some music in the jet tub. Roughly mixing up all the fragranced bath gels provided by the facility, I created my 'man-bath' and grabbed one of those magazines on the bedside tables. "Will you join me in the bath *Abakumah Payin?*" I asked after changing into one of the fancy bath robes hanging beside the bathroom doors. *"I have already spent about two hours in that thing...no thanks, dear."* She was right to have turned down my offer because there was something wrong with the bath I had set. The bath salts failed to effervesce before I hopped into the tub. Each ball of salt pierced into my skin and created some mild discomfort till they began to effervesce against my skin, creating a whole new good-feel sensation throughout the rest of the soak time.

We took a leisurely walk through the trails in the woods through to the neighbouring White memorial wildlife conservation, which houses hiking trails that goes all the way to the tops of a nearby mountain. About 6 minutes into the walk, I said 'nope,' I had forgotten it was past our lunchtime. We had to make a quick return to the restaurant to explore and dig into the lunch menus.

The menus at the restaurant were created from the farm's fresh produce. Each farm-to-table herb and vegetable came together to create various dishes, each with its distinctive flavour and taste. Accompanied by an eclectic selection of wines, said to have been assembled from 137 countries, we proceeded to dig into the served starter. Is there a scientific explanation as to why cheese goes well with wine? The mozzarella sticks starter sat well with one of the many wines we had selected. For the main meal, we opted for the grilled chicken paillard with vegetable bouquetiere, the last on the lunch menu. Hats off to the chef! The chicken… well grilled with present moisture, a mixture of the spice and olive oils it had been bathed with on the grill. To complete our full course lunch, I had an apple cheesecake for dessert while Sarah opted for the milk chocolate Namelaka. It was a remarkable culinary experience. Each meal was served on time and at the right temperature. None of the items served on the menu was too hot or too cold. It was simple yet artsy and classy.

# Chapter 20

# Chapter 20

We took the next vacation home, again around summertime 2019, before the lockdown disrupted the goings and comings of our lives the subsequent year. The luxurious Royal Senchi, the 4-star beauty standing on 35 acres of lush greenery with a stunning view of the River Volta. It was the ideal location for all who sought real romance and relaxation. The ultimate setting in all of West Africa to manifest your vacation desires. Before driving to Akosombo from the Airport, we headed straight to Oyarifa to see my mother. My Ghana had changed so much from my days at Golden Tulip. Tall buildings erupted everywhere, comprising office complexes, hotels, apartments and shopping malls. The roads looked smoother than they did in my young struggling days. The streets of Accra, specifically from the Airport shell, Spintex, Opeibea Junction, and East Legon areas had seen a significant splash of sophistication. Of course, I had been here in previous years to work, but this was the first time I was mentally present on a trip to my homeland — to take in all the changes and beauty.

I pictured a school— Fransar Catering School on the vast empty lands by the Oyarifa-Aburi main roadside. An institution which would nurture the wild untapped culinary talents in young men and women who only lived the life they truly deserve in the depths of their minds. An institution which would support the dreams of young overachievers like me, who had little to no support from family, and possibly, help launch and establish their careers in the next phase of their lives. What would the motto be? I hadn't given it that much deep thought, but I believe it would be something which would ring with "every dream is valid."

Ma had something prepared for us. She said that fish light soup was a herbal remedy to relieve the average Ghanaian of stress from labour and travels. I had never heard of that but she wasn't wrong either. We seemed a bit more relaxed after the warm bowl of fish light soup. The driver of the rented car we had booked for our trip waited outside the enclosed compound with our luggage. How trusting. The only bag we brought inside with us was the one that contained the goodies we got for Ma.

She smiled at us for minutes without saying a word. Knowing her, I believed it was her expression of gladness. She fought hard to hold back her tears as she broke the silence in Ga, *'My son, my blood, my seed now dwells and rubs shoulders with the Americans in their land. Handling his own business with his wife and children. My hard-headed Joojo has finally made it; today he has brought me plenty of items I didn't even ask for… my heart is pleased."* I broke right into tears. The past quickly came running back to me, the hunger, humiliation, the passing of my brother and the ridicules we spent our childhood combating. I sat before that day, not as a teenager seeking school fees or enquiring about what we were going to eat, but as an accomplished man, a married one with his wife, who had come bearing gifts for the woman whose faith and prayers had made it all possible. We had intentionally opted for a flight, scheduled to arrive in Accra as early as 7 am, to make it in time to see Ma and head for our getaway at Royal Senchi Akosombo.

We departed from Oyarifa at about 1 pm to make our way to our luxury stay at the Royal Senchi. I had read that the 35-acre property had been designed to take advantage of God's gift of refreshment to the Eastern Region...The Volta River. Within two hours, we arrived at the location with a concierge on-site and already assigned to us.

Our river view suite, all 63 square meters of it, aside from having a breathtaking view of the Volta River, had a spacious living room and a bedroom designed to inspire and meet every need. The air was fresh, cleaner than that which blew through the country's main capital. Our suite came with an all-inclusive breakfast, a complimentary welcome drink, of course, free wifi, access to non-motorized water sports, a large lounge area within the suite and 24-hour room service. Signing up for the River view Suite granted us access to the tennis and golf rang All 84 rooms had spectacular views with their distinct architectural design, mingling with styles of traditional and modern Ghana, proving the highest international standard of comfort.

The most impressive thing to me about the establishment was not its architecture. Yes, it sat in green magnificence but mine was the humanity and/or empathy behind its staff recruitment. 70% of its workforce was from the Asuogyaman district, which consisted of Akosombo and its surrounding environs, the locals who did not have mandatory knowledge about working in the hospitality industry were provided with training to fit into the vision of the Hotel, which was "to be the topmost hotel in Ghana with international standards." For those who struggled with the English language, the management fully sponsored English proficiency courses for those selected people from the locality. thereby giving back to the community by reducing the rate of unemployment. Due to their acts of humanity, the Asuogyaman district had become some sort of a covering for the establishment as they continue to support and give back to the local community.

Now, this is the kind of place I wouldn't blink twice about spending my money or indulging in whatever activity they presented to me, knowing that the cash going outflow was in a way going to aid in increasing productivity, especially among the Ghanaian youth. From 'hello' to 'goodbye', our stay at the Royal Senchi was an absolute pleasure. Our one-week stay was characterized by boat rides, tennis, golfing, long walks in nature, swimming and a simple picnic. You should know by now that, I wouldn't go any further in my narrations without talking about my cuisine explorations at the Senchi.

Fine dining at the restaurant breathed elegance. From every bite to every sip under the beaming mushroom lights, one could not help but stay fully present in this spectacular dining experience. A soft saxophone tune from the in-built wall speakers echoed gently through the halls of the well-lit restaurant. For our first dinner sitting at the hotel, we had ordered a Sauvignon Blanc to toast to safe travels and good times ahead. In about 20 minutes, the waiter carried in his left palm the tray which held our nourishments for the night. The grilled garlic shrimp I had ordered came with a side of spinach and fried rice, while Sarah's grouper fillet came with lemon butter sauce and steamed rice. From the first chew, I could tell that the shrimps were very well marinated in a garlic sauce and grilled carefully in their shells. The good bite was accompanied by the expected "Mmm" ... a signal of pure bliss in my mouth. The shrimp had hit the right spot as the garlic blended well with the paprika and smoke from the grill. That shrimp was worth travelling for. The fried rice... not so much. It had tasted quite ordinary and the pricing was decent. Sarah's white fish had a moist and firm texture with a mild to moderate flavour. It went well with the lemon butter sauce which made her consume the side of steamed rice with ease. In all I'd say that our first dining experience was amazing—

the food spectacular —the atmosphere fantastic and the wait staff, polite and excellent. I'm not too big on seafood but that shrimp could have me coming back for more.

The mid-morning cruise on the Volta River the next day was incredible. The beautiful scenes of fauna and flora on board the Harris boat on the river were one to remember. The cruise went ride under the Adomi Bridge and straight to the famous Akosombo Dam. Driving on top of the Adomi Bridge was nice. The feeling derived from going right underneath it was inexplicable. It was as if the closer we got, the more life-like the bridge appeared. The *wows* and the *yums* on the boat made it all enjoyable from start to finish. Our faces hugged the winds at every turn while the designated DJ on board turned on the soulful voice of Nigeria's Simi on her *smile for me* song. It went well with the mood on the boat. I pulled Sarah closer and faked a waltz to the tune. It was perfect. The ambience, the music. Casting my mind back to our early days in America, when we rummaged through the affluent dumps of Maryland, I had always hoped for days like this. Days where I'd carry my lady on trips around the world and watch her loosen up from the grips of the hustle. I looked up to give thanks to God for keeping me alive to witness that day.

We soaked for 15 minutes together in the tub and settled into the living room in the suite for some TV time. No Fransar talks, it was all jokes and laughter… recollecting memories from the adventures of the past hours on the boat. We called in to check with our kids who were being watched by Aunty Ruby. Yes, my favourite aunty had relocated to Virginia, where she lived with her two daughters, Nana Ama Oduro and Ewura Abena Oduro. Our children wanted us to trust in their independence and allow them to run the affairs of the home and watch over themselves.

"But we aren't kids anymore. Why does Aunty Ruby have to watch us? I can cook and cater for myself and the boys till you return from vacation. Trust me, dad, I've got this." said my not-so-little Cecilia. I never doubted her sense of maturity and her ability to run the home. Mine was more of a safety concern.

The remainder of our time at the Senchi before embarking on our flight back to Maryland, USA, was filled with reading by the pool, playing couples' tennis with my wife and another visiting couple we had met, and watching birds and butterflies at the little green area before the river and watching the sun succumb to darkness. It felt safe and like home. The concierge requested that we tried the banku and tilapia the restaurant was well-known for its unique tilapia flavouring. With less than 24 hours to departure, Sarah and I sat again at the restaurant for what would be our final heavy meal at the establishment. The meal was served on a well-carved wooden platter, which directly held the tilapia, neatly garnished with onions, green pepper and tomatoes. and the mini earthenware bowls which had the red and green pepper sauces. The banku came heavily in its separate earthenware bowl, placed next to a wooden platter. They played Ghana's Kojo Antwi's *'Amirika'* this time at the restaurant. How strategic! The meal we were about to dig in required no diplomacy. It demanded *'Amirika'* to truly enjoy. The concierge was good to have recommended the meal. Banku and tilapia was just that! But, whoever the chef was, made it a point to make that of Senchi one to remember. The tilapia melted gracefully with every bite, going well with the freshly grounded pepper and the stream of spicy sauce it laid. The banku was well made, perfectly without lumps. I got sold by the higher ratio of corn to cassava dough in the mixture, making it suitable for all consumers. The Royal Senchi treated us well. To life, to peace, to bliss and in some ways a new beginning. We exited the grounds with all stress in the rear as we got on board the car rental for the 90-minute drive to the Kotoka International Airport.

# Chapter 21

# Chapter 21

**REFRESHED** was my feeling as I drove out of our Burtonsville home to Maple wood park place. Ambassador Pobee had called earlier to check on us and had also requested my presence at the embassy of Ghana. She had come to meet me in Washington to discuss properly, the arrangements for that year's UN General Assembly. They were at the time, preparing to host Otumfour Asantehene at the 13$^{th}$ UN General Assembly in September of that year. As you have come to know, I had mentioned in the previous part that Otumfour had been invited to give a speech on culture. It was the perfect time to take up humongous tasks because my body had been revitalized for the job ahead.

My superiors at the Maple wood park place seemed delighted to have had me back in the kitchen. "Francis took a bit of us with him when left, didn't he?" said my manager with a cheerful grin. The *hellos, how are yous* coupled with the hand waves and admirable stares gave me a slight feeling of what it probably felt like to be president or even of British royalty. I slid into my duties and continued to perform as if I had never left.

And then came the global pandemic. Nose masks, lockdown, a ban on flights and movement restrictions. I lay in bed, with every news on rising death tolls, making my stomach turn. The **COVID-19** pandemic was nothing like we had seen. No meeting of customers to plan elaborate weddings and parties, no going to church to meet and socialize with friends, no hugging.

Just empty months with a lot of hand washing and sanitizing. The world had gone wild with silence.

Luckily, couriers were among the few categories of people who were allowed to work. We moved all cooking from the kitchen rental again to our backyard to cater for the surprising rushing orders we continued to receive. The internet, utilized wisely, could be God's blessing to mankind. Working as the executive chef at the luxury assisted living facility in Maryland, I was granted mobility exemption because I was considered a key worker to the government. With this, we continued to earn and keep the business afloat. I recall the week before the first official lockdown, the nation had gone insane. Fighting one another at supermarkets for snacks and tissue paper, forgetting that the virus' main point of spread was using human contact. Shops were looted in some communities with people senselessly getting injured.

The deafening silence on the street gave me a feel of the end time. Even the number of homeless folks had dwindled. To think that my life was highly dependent on a sheet across my face terrified me. The children stayed home, away from their peers and school. Now, they all stood to keep Fransar's delivery services going. We had many large family-sized orders for a variety of meals, for some, a pack of everything on our menu was just right. God was faithful to His promise in Psalm 91 that *a thousand shall fall at thy side and ten thousand at thy right hand. it shall not come nigh thee*. And it indeed didn't. Yet, I failed to ignore how we had missed sitting face-to-face our regulars and potentials, discussing business as usual. It was without a doubt a trying period for the entire world. We stood alone together, to combat a common enemy.

*The day we all turned strangers
was the day we saw each other from across the street
yet we could neither hug nor give our highs and low fives.
It was the time I heard that you were ill
but could only visit, on a condition to be separated by a thick
glass. Like mimes, we said our "I love yous" with hand signs
and by the manipulations of our lips.*

*The day we all turned strangers
was the day you called over video when you only lived a mile
away. Side-by-side, we craved to sit,
yet we could not risk breathing in the same air.*

*The day we turned strangers
was the day the world went mad.
Another man even told me through the flat screen
that it was forbidden to give you that high five you liked.
He said it was safer if I sent an emoji instead...so I did.*

*The day we turned strangers was the day I saw you ache.
With every cough and cry, I saw what it was like to have
an invisible enemy squeeze away your every breath.
Helplessly I stood with nothing to do.
Fearing that helping you, would be killing me.
With each passing day of growing separation,
we were faced with the ugly realization of how granted
we had taken each other.*

*The day we turned strangers
was the day they locked us down to stew in fear,
left with nothing but an embrace of our ugly thoughts.
Waiting to hear on how many had passed or
if salvation was to come*

A penned note of how I truly perceived the global dark phenomena and how it had affected the normalcy of life as I had known it.

Each morning as I exited Burtonsville to Maplewood, Bethesda, I prayed for some solution. Even for the scientists to make headway in some discovery that could save lives and erase this new world from our minds. As the lockdown stayed longer than we had hoped, I struggled in getting acquainted with the new normal. The effort to stay connected to the force that was higher than me, to keep me sane for the sake of my family, became a struggle too. We kept away from the church society because the government said so. But the faith — the optimism— in knowing that things will someday take a turn for the better, kept my hopes up. It was Prayer, the shield of faith and a K95 mask every day.

Today, in 2022, I get to freely walk and hug my clients again. We get to say I love you and show it, in the most physical ways we can. Fransar keeps evolving and staying abreast with the dynamics of time.

In the living room of my mother's Oyarifa home, hangs a photograph of me and my family. A humbling fact which continues to push me to continue making her proud. Looking at my childhood, I doubted that I could live to accomplish anything worth celebrating or even writing about.

At that lovely picture, she looks each waking day to shower words of prayer to God on our behalf. Out of brokenness, I was formed. Without the guidance of a father, I navigated my way to becoming Executive Chef Francis Otoo and CEO of a thriving enterprise. My optimism fueled by anger and rebellion, by the grace of God, fetched me a seat at the high table. I have learnt over the years that there is absolutely nothing that I can't do with

Christ in my vessel. I am an ordinary *Nshona* boy from South Labadi Ghana West Africa, who hustled every day to make ends meet and to be accepted by a society governed greatly by discrimination…based on financial status. What I didn't allow myself to become, was greedy with no regard for humanity. From a place like mine, it was to eat or be eaten… it was easy to want to trample over the shoulders of others to climb up the ladder of success. But I knew better than to become an image of something I was strongly confronted by, on my way up.

Today, by the grace of God, if I have made it to the office of the Executive Chef at the embassy of Ghana, the official caterer of the UN General Assembly for the African community, the distinguished premises of various National embassies in America, to serve Presidents and Royals, then you, reading this should know, that your dream, no matter how old, is still valid. What would I say to the seventeen-year-old me at Ho Polytechnic? "Calm down…it all works out in the end." And as to what happens next in my story, well… it is still being written.

*The essence of my being in a single shot. (L-R): Francis Otoo Jnr, Cecilia Otoo, Gilbert Otoo and Mrs. Sarah Otoo.*

*Major milestone; Gilbert graduates from St. Vincent Pallotti High School in Maryland.*

*At Paint Branch High School in Fairland, Maryland when Francis Otoo jnr. graduated with distinction.*

*As with every milestone, the Otoos gather to celebrate and show support to one another.*

*Cecelia plays with ease, the role of a big sister to Francis Jnr. Sarah beams with pride in this photo from Junior's graduation.*

*A meaningful shot of the Otoo gentlemen.*

CPSIA information can be obtained
at www.ICGtesting.com
Printed in the USA
BVHW051648070423
661964BV00008B/290